ABSOLUTE DUTY TO GOD

Exploring moral obligations

AF528424

SØREN KIERKEGAARD
CALEB SINCLARD

Published by
GRAPEVINE BOOKS

www.grapevinebooks.com
email: contact@grapevinebooks.com

Ordering Information:
Quantity sales: Special discounts are available on quantity purchases by corporations, associations, and others.
For details, reach out to the publisher.

First published by Grapevine Books, 2025
Copyright © Grapevine, 2025
All rights reserved

Contents

Absolute Duty to God: Exploring Moral Obligations

The ethical is the universal and as such, in turn, the divine. It is therefore correct to say that all duty is ultimately duty to God; but if one cannot say more one says in effect that really I have no duty to God. The duty becomes duty to God by being referred to God, but I do not enter into relation with God in the duty itself. Thus it is a duty to love one's neighbour; it is a duty in so far as it is referred to God; yet it is not God that I come in relation to in the duty but the neighbour I love. If, in this connection, I then say that it is my duty to love God, I in fact only utter a tautology, in so far as 'God' is understood in an altogether abstract sense as the divine: i.e. the universal, i.e. duty. The whole of human existence is in that case entirely self-enclosed, as a sphere, and the ethical is at once the limit and completion. God becomes an invisible, vanishing point, an impotent thought, and his power is to be found only in the ethical, which fills all existence. So if it should occur to someone to want to love God in some other sense than that mentioned, he is merely being extravagant and loves a phantom which, if it only had the strength to speak, would say to him: 'Stay where you belong, I don't ask for your love.' If it should occur to someone to want to love God in another way, this love would be suspect, like the love referred to by Rousseau when he talks of a person's loving the Kaffirs instead of his neighbour.

Now if all this is correct, if there is nothing incommensurable in a human life, but any incommensurability were due only to some chance from which nothing followed so far as existence is looked at in light of the Idea, then Hegel would be right. But where he is wrong is in talking about faith or in letting Abraham be looked on as its father; for in this latter he has passed sentence both on Abraham and on faith. In the Hegelian philosophy das Äussere (die Entäusserung) [the outer, the externalization] is higher than das Innere [the inner]. This is often illustrated by an example. The child is das Innere, the man das Äussere; which is why the child is determined precisely by the outer, and conversely the man as das Äussere by the inner. Faith, on the contrary, is this paradox, that interiority is higher than exteriority, or to recall again an expression we used above, that the odd number is higher than the even.

In the ethical view of life, then, it is the individual's task to divest himself of the determinant of interiority and give it an expression in the exterior. Whenever the individual shrinks from doing so, whenever he wants to stay inside, or slip back into, the inner determinant of feeling, mood, etc., he commits an offence, he is in a state of temptation. The paradox of faith is this, that there is an interiority that is incommensurable with the exterior, an interiority which, it should be stressed, is not identical with the first [that of the child], but is a new interiority. This must not be overlooked. Recent philosophy has allowed itself without further ado to substitute the immediate for 'faith'. If one does that it is ridiculous to deny that faith has existed through all ages. Faith in such a case keeps fairly ordinary company, it belongs with feeling, mood, idiosyncrasy, hysteria and the rest. So far philosophy is right to say one should not stop at that. But there is nothing to warrant philosophy's speaking in this manner. Prior to faith there is a movement of infinity, and only then enters faith, nec opinate [unexpectedly], on the strength of the absurd. This I am very well able to understand, without claiming thereby to have faith. If faith is no more than what philosophy passes it off as then Socrates himself already went further, much further, rather than the converse, that he didn't come that far. He made the movement of infinity intellectually. His ignorance is the infinite resignation. That task is in itself a match for human strength, even if people nowadays scorn it; yet it is only when this has been done, only when the individual has exhausted himself in the infinite, that he reaches the point where faith can emerge.

Then faith's paradox is this, that the single individual is higher than the universal, that the single individual (to recall a theological distinction less in vogue these days) determines his relation to the universal through his relation to the absolute, not his relation to the absolute through his relation to the universal. The paradox can also be put by saying that there is an absolute duty to God; for in this tie of obligation the individual relates himself absolutely, as the single individual, to the absolute. When people now say that it is a duty to love God, it is in a sense quite different from the above; for if this duty is absolute the ethical is reduced to the relative. It doesn't follow, nevertheless, that [the ethical] is to be done away with. Only that it gets a quite different expression, the paradoxical expression, so that, e.g., love of God can cause the knight of faith to give his love of his neighbour the opposite expression to that which is his duty ethically speaking.

Unless this is how it is, faith has no place in existence; and faith is then a temptation, and Abraham is done for, since he gave in to it.

This paradox does not allow of mediation: for it rests precisely on the single individual's being only the single individual. As soon as this individual wants to express his absolute duty in the universal, becomes conscious of it in the latter, he knows he is in a state of temptation, and then, even if he otherwise resists the temptation, he does not come to fulfil that so-called absolute duty, and if he does not resist it he sins even if realiter [independently of his inclination, wishes, state of mind] his act is the one that was his absolute duty. Thus what could Abraham have done? If he had wanted to say to someone: 'I love Isaac more than everything in the world, and that's why it is so hard for me to sacrifice him', the person would surely have shaken his head and said: 'Then why sacrifice him?', or if he was a perceptive fellow perhaps he might even have seen through Abraham, realized that he was betraying feelings which stood in flagrant contradiction with his deed.

In the story of Abraham we find just such a paradox. Ethically speaking his relation to Isaac is this, that the father is to love the son. This ethical relationship is reduced to the relative as against the absolute relation to God. To the question, why?, Abraham has no other answer than that it is a trial and a temptation, which, as remarked above, is what makes it a unity of being for both God's sake and his own. These two are also correlative in ordinary usage. Thus when we see someone do something that doesn't conform with the universal, we say, 'He can hardly be doing that for the sake of God', meaning by this that he did it for his own sake. The paradox of faith has lost the intermediate term, i.e. the universal. On the one hand it contains the expression of extreme egoism (doing this dreadful deed for his own sake) and on the other the expression of the most absolute devotion (doing it for God's sake). Faith itself cannot be mediated into the universal, for in that case it would be cancelled. Faith is this paradox, and the single individual is quite unable to make himself intelligible to anyone. One might suppose the single individual could make himself understood to another individual who is in the same situation. Such a view would be unthinkable were it not that nowadays people try in so many ways to sneak their way into greatness. The one knight of faith simply cannot help the other. Either the single individual becomes a knight of faith himself by putting on the paradox, or he never becomes one. Partnership in these regions is quite unthinkable. If there is any more precise explanation of the idea behind the sacrifice of Isaac, it is one that the individual can only give to himself. And supposing one could settle, even with some exactitude, in universal terms, how to understand the case of Isaac (which would in any case be the most absurd self-contradiction, namely that the single individual who stands precisely outside the universal be brought in under universal categories, when he is expressly to act as the single individual outside the universal), the individual could still never be assured of [the truth of] this explanation by others, but only by himself as the single individual. So even if someone were so cowardly and base as to want to be a knight of faith on someone else's responsibility, he would never become one; for only the single individual becomes one, as the single individual, and this is the knight's greatness, as I can well understand without being party to it, since I lack courage; though also his terror, as I can understand even better.

As everyone knows, Luke 14.26 presents a remarkable teaching on the absolute duty to God: 'If any man come to me, and hate not his father, and mother, and wife, and children, and brethren, and sisters, yea, and his own life also, he cannot be my disciple.' This is a hard saying, who can bear to hear it? And for that reason it is heard very seldom. Yet this silence is only a futile evasion. The student of theology learns, however, that these words occur in the New Testament, and in one or another exegetical aid he finds the information that misein [to hate], both here and in some other passages, is used per meiosin [by adopting a weaker sense] to mean: minus diligo [love less], posthabeo [give less priority to], non colo [show no respect to], nihil facio [make nothing of]. The context in which these words occur seems, however, not to corroborate this tasteful explanation. For in the next verse [but one] there is a story about someone who plans to erect a tower but first makes some estimate of his capacity to do so, lest he be the object of ridicule later. The close link between this story and the verse quoted seems to suggest precisely that the words are to be taken in as terrifying a sense as possible in order that everyone should examine his own ability to erect the building.

If this pious and tender-minded exegete, who thinks he can smuggle Christianity into the world by haggling in this way, should succeed in convincing anyone that grammatically, linguistically, and kata analogian [by analogy] this was the meaning of the passage, then it is to be hoped that in so doing he also manages to convince the same person that Christianity is one of the most miserable things in the world. For the teaching which in one of its most lyrical outpourings, where the sense of its eternal validity swells up most strongly, has nothing to offer but a sounding phrase that signifies nothing and suggests only that one is to be less kind, less attentive, more indifferent; the teaching which, just as it seems to want to tell us something terrible, ends up in drivel rather than terror — that teaching is certainly not worth standing up for.

The words are terrible, but I feel sure they can be understood without the person who understands them necessarily having the courage to do as they say. And yet there must be honesty enough to admit what is there, to confess to its greatness even if one lacks the courage oneself. Anyone who manages that will not exclude himself from a share in the beautiful story, for in a way it contains a kind of comfort for the man who lacks courage to begin building the tower. But he must be honest and not pass off this lack of courage as humility, since on the contrary it is pride, while the courage of faith is the only humble courage.

One now sees readily that if the passage is to have any sense, it must be understood literally. It is God who demands absolute love. Anyone who, in demanding a person's love, thinks this must be proved by the latter's becoming lukewarm towards all that was hitherto dear to him, is not simply an egoist but a fool, and anyone demanding such a love would simultaneously sign his own death-warrant in so far as his life is bound up in this love he craves. A husband requires his wife to leave her father and mother, but were he to regard it as proof of her special love for him that for his sake she became a lukewarm, indolent daughter, etc., then he would be an idiot among idiots. Had he any notion of what love was, he would want to discover — and should he discover it see in this an assurance that his wife loved him more than any other in the kingdom — that she was perfect in her love as daughter and sister. So what would be considered a sign of egoism and stupidity in a person, one is supposed with the help of an exegete to regard as a worthy conception of the deity.

But how then hate them? I shall not take up the human love/hate distinction here, not because I have so much against it, since at least it is a passionate distinction, but it is egoistic and so does not fit here. If I regard the requirement as a paradox, on the other hand, then I understand it, i.e. understand it in the way one can understand a paradox. The absolute duty can then lead to what ethics would forbid, but it can by no means make the knight of faith have done with loving. This is shown by Abraham. The moment he is ready to sacrifice Isaac, the ethical expression for what he does is this: he hates Isaac. But if he actually hates Isaac he can be certain that God does not require this of him; for Cain and Abraham are not the same. Isaac he must love with all his soul. When God asks for Isaac, Abraham must if possible love him even more, and only then can he sacrifice him; for it is indeed this love of Isaac that in its paradoxical opposition to his love of God makes his act a sacrifice. But the distress and anguish in the paradox is that, humanly speaking, he is quite incapable of making himself understood. Only in the moment when his act is in absolute contradiction with his feeling, only then does he sacrifice Isaac, but the reality of his act is that in virtue of which he belongs to the universal, and there he is and remains a murderer.

Furthermore, the passage in Luke must be understood in such a way that one grasps that the knight of faith has no higher expression whatever of the universal (as the ethical) which can save him. Thus if we imagine the Church were to demand this sacrifice of one of its members, then all we have is a tragic hero. For qualitatively the idea of the Church is no different from that of the State, inasmuch as the individual can enter it by common mediation, and in so far as the individual has entered the paradox he does not arrive at the idea of the Church; he doesn't get out of the paradox either, but must find either his blessedness or his damnation inside it. An ecclesiastical hero expresses the universal in his deed, and no one in the Church, not even his father or mother, etc., will fail to understand him. But he is not the knight of faith, and has also a different answer from Abraham's; he doesn't say it is a trial or a temptation in which he is being tested.

One as a rule refrains from citing texts like the one in Luke. There is a fear of letting people loose, a fear that the worst will happen once the individual enjoys carrying on like an individual. Moreover living as the individual is thought to be the easiest thing of all, and it is the universal that people must be coerced into becoming. I can share neither this fear nor this opinion, and for the same reason. No person who has learned that to exist as the individual is the most terrifying thing of all will be afraid of saying it is the greatest. But then he mustn't say it in a way that makes his words a pitfall for somebody on the loose, but rather in a way that helps that person into the universal, even though his words can make some small allowance for greatness. The person who dares not mention such passages dares not mention Abraham either, and to think that existing as the individual is an easy enough matter implies a very dubious indirect admission with regard to oneself; for someone who really respects himself and is concerned for his own soul is assured of the fact that a person living under his own supervision in the world at large lives in greater austerity and seclusion than a maiden in her lady's bower. That there may be some who need coercion, who if given free rein would riot in selfish pleasure like unbridled beasts, is no doubt true, but one should show precisely by the fact that one knows how to speak with fear and trembling that one is not of their number. And out of respect for greatness one should indeed speak, lest it be forgotten for fear of the harm which surely won't arise if one speaks as one who knows it is the great, knows its terrors, and if one doesn't know these one doesn't know its greatness either.

Let us then consider more closely the distress and fear in the paradox of faith. The tragic hero renounces himself in order to express the universal; the knight of faith renounces the universal in order to be the particular. As mentioned, it all depends on how one is placed. Someone who believes it is a simple enough matter to be the individual can always be certain that he is not the knight of faith; for stragglers and vagrant geniuses are not men of faith. Faith's knight knows on the contrary that it is glorious to belong to the universal. He knows it is beautiful and benign to be the particular who translates himself into the universal, the one who so to speak makes a clear and elegant edition of himself, as immaculate as possible, and readable for all; he knows it is refreshing to become intelligible to oneself in the universal, so that he understands the universal and everyone who understands him understands the universal through him in turn, and both rejoice in the security of the universal. He knows it is beautiful to be born as the particular with the universal as his home, his friendly abode, which receives him straightaway with open arms when he wishes to stay there. But he also knows that higher up there winds a lonely path, narrow and steep; he knows it is terrible to be born in solitude outside the universal, to walk without meeting a single traveller. He knows very well where he is, and how he is related to men.

Humanly speaking he is insane and cannot make himself understood to anyone. And yet 'insane' is the mildest expression for him. If he isn't viewed thus, he is a hypocrite and the higher up the path he climbs, the more dreadful a hypocrite he becomes.

The knight of faith knows it gives inspiration to surrender oneself to the universal, that it takes courage to do so, but also that there is a certain security in it, just because it is for the universal; he knows it is glorious to be understood by every noble mind, and in such a way that even the beholder is thereby ennobled. This he knows and he feels as though bound, he could wish this was the task he had been set. Thus surely Abraham must have now and then wished that the task was to love Isaac in a way meet and fitting for a father, as all would understand and as would be remembered for all time; he must have wished his task was to sacrifice Isaac for the universal, so as to inspire fathers to illustrious deeds - and he must have been well nigh horrified by the thought that for him such wishes were merely temptations and must be treated as such; for he knew it was a solitary path he trod, and that he was doing nothing for the universal but only being tested and tried himself. Or what was it Abraham did for the universal? Let me speak humanly about it, really humanly! It takes him seventy years to get the son of his old age. What others get soon enough and have long joy of takes him seventy years. And why? Because he is being tested and tried. Is that not insanity? But Abraham believed, and only Sarah wavered and got him to take Hagar as his concubine — but for that reason he also had to drive Hagar away. He gets Isaac and now he is to be tried once again. He knew it was glorious to express the universal, glorious to live with Isaac. But this is not the task. He knew it would have been a kingly deed to sacrifice such a son for the universal, he himself would have found repose in that, and everyone would have 'reposed' in their praise of his deed, just as the vowel 'reposes' in its quiescent letter; but this is not the task — he is being tried. That Roman general famous under the name of Cunctator halted the enemy by his delaying tactics, yet what kind of delayer is Abraham by comparison? But he isn't saving the State. This is the sum of one hundred and thirty years. Who can bear it? Should his contemporaries — if they can be called that — not say: 'There is an eternal procrastinating with Abraham; when he finally gets a son — and that took long enough — he wants to sacrifice him; he must be demented; and if only he could explain why he wanted to do that, but no, it's always a "trial" '? Nor could Abraham offer any further explanation, for his life is like a book put under divine seizure and which will never become publici juris [public property].

This is what is terrible. Anyone who doesn't see this can always be quite certain he is no knight of faith; but anyone who does see it will not deny that the step of even the most tried tragic hero goes like a dance compared with the slow and creeping progress of the knight of faith. And having seen it and realized he does not have the courage to understand it, he must at least have some idea of the wonderful glory achieved by that knight in becoming God's confidant, the Lord's friend, and — to speak really humanly — in addressing God in heaven as 'Thou', while even the tragic hero only addresses him in the third person.

The tragic hero is soon finished, his struggle is soon at an end; he makes the infinite movement and is now safe in the universal. But the knight of faith is kept awake, for he is under constant trial and can turn back in repentance to the universal at any moment, and this possibility can just as well be a temptation as the truth. Enlightenment as to which is something he can get from no one; otherwise he would be outside the paradox.

The knight of faith has therefore, first and foremost, the passion to concentrate the whole of the ethical that he violates in one single thing; he can be sure that he really loves Isaac with all his soul.5 If he cannot be that, he is in a state of temptation. Next, he has the passion to evoke this certainty intact in a twinkling and in as fully valid a way as in the first instance. If he cannot do this he doesn't get started, for then he must constantly start again from the beginning. The tragic hero, too, concentrates in one single thing the ethical that he teleologically violates, but in this thing he has resort to the universal. The knight of faith has only himself, and it is there the terrible lies. Most people let their ethical obligations last a day at a time, but then they never reach this passionate concentration, this energetic awareness. The tragic hero can in a sense be helped by the universal in acquiring these, but the knight of faith is alone about everything. The tragic hero acts and finds his point of rest in the universal, the knight of faith is kept in constant tension. Agamemnon gives up his claim to Iphigenia, thereby finds his point of rest in the universal, and now proceeds to give her in sacrifice. If Agamemnon had not made the movement, if in the decisive moment, instead of a passionate concentration, his soul had been lost in common chatter about his having several daughters, and vielleicht das Ausserordentliche [perhaps something extraordinary] could happen - then naturally he would not be a hero but a case for charity. Abraham has the hero's concentration too, even though in him it is much more difficult since he has no resort at all to the universal, but he makes one movement more through which he concentrates his soul back upon the marvel. If Abraham hadn't done that he would only have been an Agamemnon, provided it can be explained how his willingness to sacrifice Isaac can be justified other than by its benefiting the universal.

Whether the individual is now really in a state of temptation or a knight of faith, only the individual can decide. Still, it is possible on the basis of the paradox to construct certain criteria which even someone not in it can understand. The true knight of faith is always absolute isolation, the false knight is sectarian. The latter involves an attempt to leap off the narrow path of the paradox in order to become a tragic hero on the cheap. The tragic hero expresses the universal and sacrifices himself for it. The sectarian Master Jackel has instead his private theatre, [i.e.] several good friends and companions who represent the universal about as well as the public witnesses in The Golden Snuffbox represent justice. The knight of faith, on the other hand, is the paradox, he is the individual, absolutely nothing but the individual, without connections and complications. This is the terror that the puny sectarian cannot endure. Instead of learning from this that he is incapable of greatness and plainly admitting it, something I cannot but approve since it is what I myself do, the poor wretch thinks he will achieve it by joining company with other poor wretches. But it won't at all work, no cheating is tolerated in the world of spirit. A dozen sectarians link arms, they know nothing at all of the lonely temptations in store for the knight of faith and which he dare not shun just because it would be more terrible still were he presumptuously to force his way forward. The sectarians deafen each other with their clang and clatter, hold dread at bay with their shrieks, and a whooping Sunday-outing like this thinks it is storming heaven, believes it is following the same path as the knight of faith who, in cosmic isolation, hears never a voice but walks alone with his dreadful responsibility.

As for the knight of faith, he is assigned to himself alone, he has the pain of being unable to make himself intelligible to others but feels no vain desire to show others the way. The pain is the assurance, vain desires are unknown to him, his mind is too serious for that. The false knight readily betrays himself by this instantly acquired proficiency; he just doesn't grasp the point that if another individual is to walk the same path he has to be just as much the individual and is therefore in no need of guidance, least of all from one anxious to press his services on others. Here again, people unable to bear the martyrdom of unintelligibility jump off the path, and choose instead, conveniently enough, the world's admiration of their proficiency. The true knight of faith is a witness, never a teacher, and in this lies the deep humanity in him which is more worth than this foolish concern for others' weal and woe which is honoured under the name of sympathy, but which is really nothing but vanity. A person who wants only to be a witness confesses thereby that no one, not even the least, needs another person's sympathy, or is to be put down so another can raise himself up. But because what he himself won he did not win on the cheap, so neither does he sell it on the cheap; he is not so pitiable as to accept people's admiration and pay for it with silent contempt; he knows that whatever truly is great is available equally for all.

So either there is an absolute duty to God, and if so then it is the paradox described, that the single individual as the particular is higher than the universal and as the particular stands in an absolute relation to the absolute - or else faith has never existed because it has existed always; or else Abraham is done for; or else one must explain the passage in Luke 14 in the way that tasteful exegete did, and explain the corresponding passages likewise, and similar ones.

Bonus Content

Fear and Trembling: A Condensed Edition

Preface

Not just in commerce but in the world of ideas too our age is putting on a veritable clearance sale. Everything can be had so dirt cheap that one begins to wonder whether in the end anyone will want to make a bid. Every speculative score-keeper who conscientiously marks up the momentous march of modem philosophy, every lecturer, crammer, student, everyone on the outskirts of philosophy or at its centre is unwilling to stop with doubting everything. They all go further. It would perhaps be malapropos to inquire where they think they are going, though surely we may in all politeness and respect take it for granted that they have indeed doubted everything, otherwise it would be odd to talk of going further. This preliminary step is one they have all of them taken, and presumably with so little effort as to feel no need to drop some word about how; for not even someone genuinely anxious for a little enlightenment on this will find such. Not a gesture that might point him in the right direction, no small dietary prescription for how to go about such a huge task. 'But Descartes did it, didn't he?' A venerable, humble, honest thinker whose writings surely no one can read without being most deeply stirred - Descartes must have done what he has said and said what he has done. A rare enough occurrence in our own time! Descartes, as he himself repeatedly insists, was no doubter in matters of faith. ('[B]ut we must keep in mind what has been said, that we must trust to this natural light only so long as nothing contrary to it is revealed by God himself ... Above all we should impress on our memory as an infallible rule that what God has revealed to us is incomparably more certain than anything else; and that we ought to submit to the Divine authority rather than to our own judgement even though the light of reason may seem to us to suggest, with the utmost clearness and evidence, something opposite' [from Principles 28 and 76 of Principles of Philosophy].) Descartes has not cried 'Fire!' and made it everyone's duty to doubt, for Descartes was a quiet and lonely thinker, not a bellowing streetwatch; he was modest enough to allow that his method was important only for himself and sprang partly from his own earlier bungling with knowledge. ('Thus my design here is not to teach the Method which everyone should follow in order to promote the good conduct of Reason, but only to show in what manner I have endeavoured to conduct my own ... But so soon as I had achieved the entire course of study [that is, of his youth - Johannes de silentio's interpolation] at the close of which one is usually received into the ranks of the learned, I entirely changed my opinion. For I found myself embarrassed with so many doubts and errors that it seemed to me that the effort to instruct myself had no effect other than the increasing discovery of my own ignorance' [Discourse on the Method of Rightly Conducting the Reason and Seeking the Truth in the Sciences].) - What those old Greeks, whom one must also credit with a little knowledge of philosophy, took to be the task of a whole lifetime, doubt not being a skill one acquires in days and weeks; what the old veteran warrior achieved after keeping the balance of doubt in the face of all inveiglements, fearlessly rejecting the certainties of sense and thought, incorruptibly defying selfish anxieties and the wheedling of sympathies - that is where nowadays everyone begins.

Today nobody will stop with faith; they all go further. It would perhaps be rash to inquire where to, but surely a mark of urbanity and good breeding on my part to assume that in fact everyone does indeed have faith, otherwise it would be odd to talk of going further. In those old days it was different. For then faith was a task for a whole lifetime, not a skill thought to be acquired in either days or weeks. When the old campaigner approached the end, had fought the good fight, and kept his faith, his heart was still young enough not to have forgotten the fear and trembling that disciplined his youth and which, although the grown man mastered it, no man altogether outgrows - unless he somehow manages at the earliest possible opportunity to go further. Where these venerable figures arrived our own age begins, in order to go further.

The present author is no philosopher, he has not understood the System, nor does he know if there really is one, or if it has been completed. As far as his own weak head is concerned the thought of what huge heads everyone must have in order to have such huge thoughts is already enough. Even if one were able to render the whole of the content of faith into conceptual form, it would not follow that one had grasped faith, grasped how one came to it, or how it came to one. The present author is no philosopher, he is poetice et eleganter [to put it in poetic and well-chosen terms], an occasional copyist who neither writes the System nor makes any promises about it, who pledges neither anything about the System nor himself to it. He writes because for him doing so is a luxury, the more agreeable and conspicuous the fewer who buy and read what he writes. In an age where passion has been done away with for the sake of science he easily foresees his fate - in an age when an author who wants readers must be careful to write in a way that he can be comfortably leafed through during the after-dinner nap, and be sure to present himself to the world like the polite gardener's boy in the Advertiser who, hat in hand and with good references from his previous place of employment, recommends himself to a much-esteemed public. He foresees his fate will be to be completely ignored; has a dreadful foreboding that the scourge of zealous criticism will more than once make itself felt; and shudders at what terrifies him even more, that some enterprising recorder, a paragraph swallower who to rescue learning is always willing to do to others' writings what, to 'preserve good taste', Trop nobly did to The Destruction of the Human Race, will slice him into sections as ruthlessly as the man who, in the service of the science of punctuation, divided up his speech by counting the words and putting a full-stop after every fifty and a semi-colon after every thirty-five. No, I prostrate myself before any systematic bag-searcher; this is not the System, it hasn't the slightest thing to do with the System. I wish all good on the System and on the Danish shareholders in that omnibus; for it will hardly become a tower. I wish them good luck and prosperity one and all.

Respectfully

Johannes de silentio

Attunement

There was a man who had heard the story of how God tested Abraham since he was a child. As he grew older, his admiration for the tale increased, yet he struggled to comprehend its meaning. His thoughts constantly returned to the story, and he yearned to have been there as a witness. His desire was not for the landscapes or the characters involved, but specifically to accompany Abraham and Isaac on their journey to the mountain in Moriah. This man was not a thinker; he found fulfillment in faith alone. He believed that being remembered as the father of faith would be the greatest glory, even if no one else knew. While he lacked knowledge of Hebrew, he believed that understanding the language might have made the story clearer to him.

I

And so it happened that God tested Abraham, telling him to offer his son Isaac as a burnt offering on a mountain in Moriah. Early in the morning, Abraham and Isaac set out on their journey, leaving Sarah behind to watch them. For three days, they rode in silence until they saw the mountain in the distance. Abraham left the servants behind and proceeded alone with Isaac. Along the way, Abraham paused and blessed Isaac, but the young boy could not understand the gravity of the situation. He pleaded with Abraham, reminding him of their life together and begging for his life. Abraham comforted him with words of encouragement, but Isaac remained oblivious.

As they reached the mountain, Abraham's fatherly expression changed, and he confessed to Isaac that it was not God's command but his own desire. Isaac trembled and cried out to God, asking for mercy. Abraham silently thanked God, accepting that it was better for Isaac to believe him a monster than to lose faith in God.

*

A mother blackens her breast when weaning a child, but the mother's tender love remains the same. Those who do not require more terrible means to separate them are truly fortunate.

II

It was early morning, and Abraham rose, embracing Sarah, his bride of old age, and Sarah kissed Isaac, her pride and hope for future generations. In silence, they rode on, with Abraham's gaze fixed on the ground. On the fourth day, he looked up and saw the mountain in Moriah from afar, but then turned his eyes back down. Silently, he prepared the firewood, bound Isaac, and silently drew the knife. However, he saw a ram appointed by God and sacrificed it instead. From that day on, Abraham aged, unable to forget what God had demanded of him, while Isaac continued to thrive. Abraham's joy was eclipsed, and he saw joy no more.

*

As a child grows and needs to be weaned, the mother covers her breast, symbolizing the separation. The child who only experiences this form of loss is truly fortunate!

III

It was early morning when Abraham rose and kissed Sarah, the young mother, and Sarah kissed Isaac, her everlasting delight. Abraham rode thoughtfully, reflecting on Hagar and the son he had sent away into the desert. He climbed the mountain in Moriah and prepared to draw the knife.

However, on a tranquil evening, he rode alone to the mountain, prostrating himself and begging God for forgiveness for his willingness to sacrifice Isaac. He rode this lonely path frequently but found no peace. He could not comprehend why it was considered a sin to offer to God the most precious thing he owned, the thing for which he would have sacrificed his own life. And if it was indeed a sin, he struggled to understand how it could be forgiven. For what sin could be more terrible?

*

When a child is to be weaned, the mother experiences sorrow as she and the child grow apart, no longer as close as before. They suffer this brief sorrow together. The one who kept the child close and did not need to sorrow further is truly fortunate.

IV

Everything was prepared for the journey. He bid farewell to Sarah, and the faithful servant Eleazar accompanied them until he had to turn back. Abraham and Isaac rode together until they reached the mountain in Moriah. There, Abraham calmly and quietly prepared for the sacrifice, but Isaac noticed the clenched anguish in Abraham's left hand and the shudder that ran through his body. Nonetheless, Abraham drew the knife.

They returned home, and Sarah ran to meet them, unaware of what had transpired. Isaac lost his faith, yet he kept silent about it, and Abraham remained unaware that anyone had witnessed it.

*

When a child is to be weaned, the mother ensures there is solid food available so that the child does not perish. The one who has such sustenance at hand is truly fortunate!

In these and similar ways, the man of whom we speak pondered those events. Whenever he returned from a journey to the mountain in Moriah, he would collapse in weariness, clasp his hands, and declare, "No one was as great as Abraham; who can understand him?"

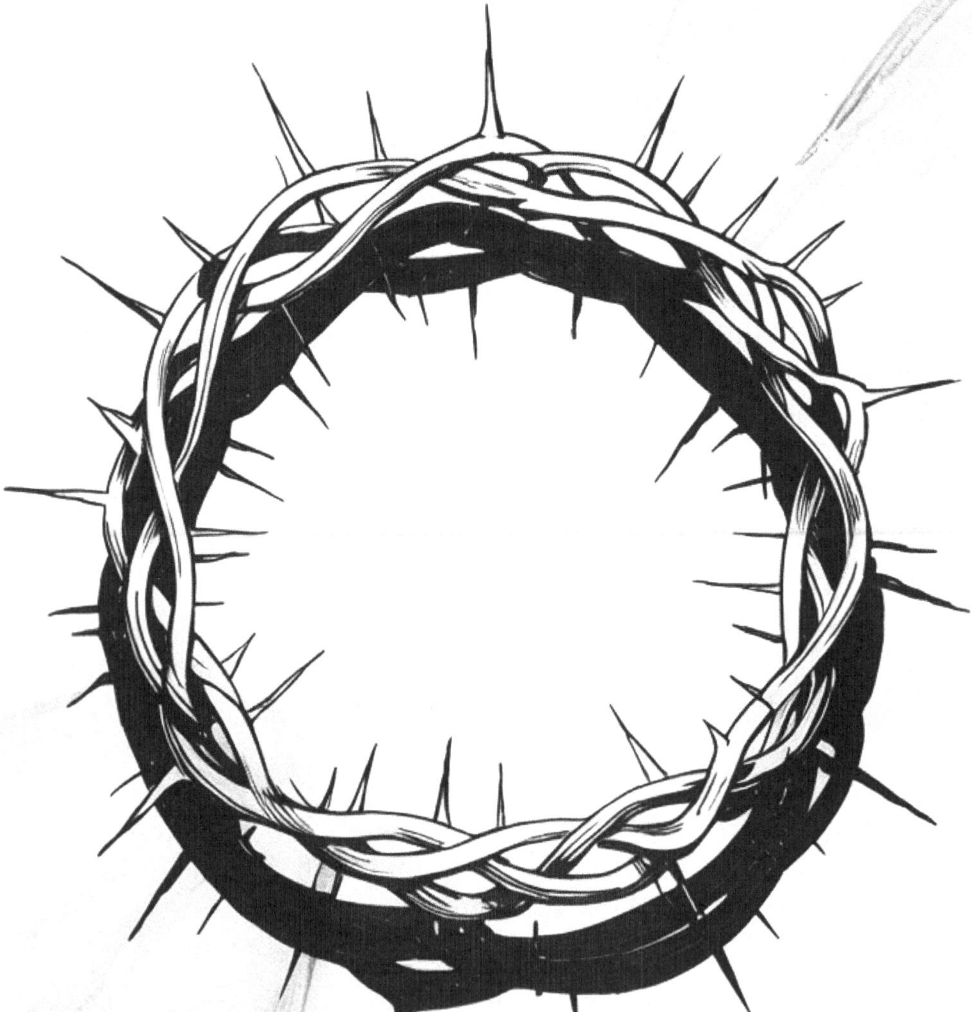

Speech in Praise of Abraham

If there were no eternal consciousness in a man, if an unfathomable, insatiable emptiness lay hid beneath everything, what would life be but despair? If there were no sacred bond uniting mankind, if one generation rose up after another like the leaves of the forest or as the songs of birds in the woods - how empty and devoid of comfort would life be! But for that reason it is not so, and as God created man and woman, so too he shaped the hero and the poet or speech-maker. The latter has none of the skills of the former, he can only admire, love, take pleasure in the hero. Yet he, too, is equally happy, and his love is one of admiration. Heis the spirit of remembrance, admiring and bringing to mind what has been done. Though he takes nothing for himself, he is devoted to his charge, spreading admiration for the hero to all. This achievement is his humble task and faithful service in the hero's house. If he remains true to his love and fights against oblivion, he fulfills his task and is united with the hero. No one great shall be forgotten.

But everyone is great in their own way; and each person's greatness is proportional to their love. Those who loved themselves, others, or God achieved greatness accordingly. They shall all be remembered based on their expectations and the magnitude of their struggles. Those who strove with the world or themselves became great, but those who strove with God became even greater. Abraham, embodying the power of powerlessness, the wisdom of folly, the hope of insanity, and the love that is self-hatred, was greater than all.

By faith Abraham could leave the land of his fathers and become a stranger in the land of promise. Otherwise would have been senseless to do so, where there was nothing to remind him of what was dear, but the novelty of everything tempted his soul to longing.

And yet he was God's chosen, in whom the Lord was well pleased! If only he had been disowned, cast out from God's grace, he would have understood it better. As it was it looked more like a mockery of himself and his faith.

There was once another who lived in. He is not forgotten, nor his songs of lament in which in sorrow he sought and found what he had lost. From Abraham we have no song of lament. It is human to complain, but it is greater to have faith and more blessed to behold the believer.

It was faith that made Abraham accept the promise that all nations of the earth should be blessed in his seed. Time went by, the possibility was still there, and Abraham had faith; time went by, it became unlikely, and Abraham had faith.

There was once another who held out an expectation. He did not forget his expectation for a long while. Then he sorrowed, and the sorrow did not deceive him as life had done. It is human to sorrow with the sorrower, but greater to have faith and more blessed to behold the believer.

From Abraham we have no song of sorrow. He did not mournfully count the days, he did not cast suspicious glances at Sarah, fearing she was growing old; he did not soothingly sing to Sarah his mournful lay. Abraham became old and Sarah was mocked in the land, and still he was God's chosen and heir to the promise.

Would it not be better, then, were he not God's chosen? What is it to be God's chosen? Is it to be denied one's youthful desire in order to have it fulfilled in old age?

But Abraham believed and held firm to the promise. Had Abraham wavered he would have renounced it. He would not have been forgotten; he would have saved many by his example. Yet he would not have become the father of faith; for it is great to give up one's desire, but greater to stick to it after having given it up.

But then came the fullness of time. Had Abraham not had faith, then Sarah would surely have died of sorrow, and Abraham, dull with grief, instead of understanding the fulfilment, would have smiled at it as at a youthful dream. But Abraham believed, and therefore he was young; for who has faith, retains eternal youth.

All praise then to that tale! Outwardly the wonder of faith is in Abraham and Sarah's being young enough for it to happen according to their expectations; in a deeper sense the wonder of faith lies in their being young enough to wish, and in faith's having preserved their wish and youthfulness. He accepted the fulfilment of the promise, he accepted it in faith, and it happened according to expectation and according to faith; for Moses struck the rock with his rod but he did not believe.

So there was rejoicing in Abraham's house when Sarah was bride on their golden-wedding day.

But it was not to remain so; Abraham was to be tried once more. He had fought with time itself and kept his faith. Now all the horrors of the struggle were to be concentrated in one moment. 'And God did tempt Abraham, and said unto him ... Take now thy son, thine only son Isaac, whom thou lovest, and get thee into the land of Moriah; and offer him there for a burnt offering upon one of the mountains which I will tell thee of.'

So all was lost, more terrible than if it had never been! So the Lord was only making sport of Abraham! Through a miracle he had made the preposterous come true, now he would see it again brought to nothing. Foolery indeed!

But Abraham did not laugh at it, as Sarah had laughed. Who is it then that snatches the staff from the old man, who is it that demands that the old man himself should break it? Is there no compassion for this venerable greybeard, none for the innocent child? And yet Abraham was God's chosen, and it was the Lord who put him to this test.

All was now surely lost! The glorious memory of the human race, the promise in Abraham's seed, it was only a whim, a fleeting thought of the Lord's, which Abraham himself must now eradicate. That sad yet still blessed hour when Abraham should concentrate his whole soul in a blessing with the power to give Isaac joy all his days - that moment was not to come! For, yes, death would divide them, but Isaac was to be its victim. And it was God who tried him.

But Abraham had faith, and had faith for this life. Had his faith only been for a future life it would indeed have been easier to cast everything aside in order to hasten out of this world. But he believed he would become old in his land, honoured among his people, blessed in his kin, eternally remembered in Isaac.

He believed the ridiculous. If Abraham had doubted - then he would have done something else, which would have been something great and glorious? He would have marched out to the mountain in Moriah, drawn the knife - he would have cried out to God: 'This sacrificeis not the best I possess; for what is an old man compared with the child of promise, but it is the best I can give.' He would have thrust the knife into his own breast. He would have been admired in the world and his name never forgotten; but it is one thing to be admired, another to be a guiding star that saves the anguished.

But Abraham had faith. He did not beg for himself; it was only when the just punishment had been proclaimed upon Sodom and Gomorrah that Abraham came forward with his prayers.

We read in those Holy Scriptures: 'And God did tempt Abraham, and said unto him, Abràham: Abraham, where are you? but Abraham answered: here I am.'

You, to whom my speech is addressed, was that the case with you? When you saw, far off, the heavy fate approaching, did you not say to the mountains, 'hide me', to the hills, 'fall on me'? Or if you were stronger, did your feet nevertheless not drag along the way?

Not so Abraham, gladly, boldly, trustingly he answered out loud 'here I am'. We read further: 'And Abraham rose up early in the morning.' My hearer! Many a father has lost his child, but then it was God, the unchangeable and inscrutable will of the Almighty, it was his hand that took it. Not so with Abraham. For him a harder trial was reserved; along with the knife the fate of Isaac was put into Abraham's own hand.

And he stood there, the old man with his only hope! But he did not doubt, he did not look in anguish to left or right, he did not challenge heaven with his prayers. And he drew the knife.

Had Abraham doubted as he stood on the mountain in Moriah, had he looked about in indecision - then he would have gone home, everything would have been as before, and yet how changed! For his withdrawal would have been a flight, his future perhaps damnation. Then he would have borne witness, not to his faith or to God's mercy, but to how dreadful was the journey to the mountain in Moriah. Abraham would not be forgotten, nor the mountain. Yet it would not be mentioned like Ararat, where the Ark came to land, but as a horror, for it was here that Abraham doubted.

Venerable Father Abraham! When you journeyed home you needed no speech of praise to console you for what was lost; for in fact you gained everything and kept Isaac.

You need no lover to snatch your memory from oblivion; for every mother-tongue commemorates you - and still you reward your lover more gloriously than anyone. You first bore witness to that tremendous passion that scorns the fearful struggle with the raging elements and the forces of creation in order to struggle with God instead - forgive him who would speak in your praise if he did not do it correctly. He spoke humbly, briefly, as is fitting; but he will never forget that you needed a hundred years to get the son of your old age, against every expectation, that you had to draw the knife before keeping Isaac; he will never forget that in one hundred and thirty years you got no further than faith.

Problemata

Preamble from the Heart

An old proverb pertaining to the outward and visible world says: 'Only one who works gets bread.' Oddly enough, the saying doesn't apply in the world to which it most properly belongs, for the outward world is subject to the law of imperfection; there it happens time and again that one who gets bread is one who does not work, that one who sleeps gets it in greater abundance than one who labours.

It is otherwise in the world of spirit. Here there prevails an eternal divine order, here it does not rain on the just and the unjust alike, here the sun does not shine on both good and evil, here only one who works gets bread, only one who draws the knife gets Isaac. He who will not work does not get bread, but will be deluded, as the gods deluded Orpheus because he was tender-hearted, not courageous, deluded him because he was a lyre-player, not a man.

Here it is no help to have Abraham as one's father; of anyone who will not work here one can say what is written about Israel's virgins, he gives birth to wind - while the one who works will give birth to his own father.

Conventional wisdom aims presumptuously to introduce into the world of spirit that same law of indifference under which the outside world groans. But then it does not get bread, it starves to death while everything is transformed into gold.

Now the story of Abraham will always be glorious, but only if we are willing to 'labour and be heavy laden'. But labour they will not, and yet they still want to understand the story. One speaks in Abraham's honour, but how? By making it a commonplace: 'his greatness was that he so loved God that he was willing to offer him the best he had.' 'Best' is a vague expression. In word and thought one can quite safely identify Isaac with the best. If the rich young man had sold all his possessions and given them to the poor, we would praise him but we would not understand even him without labour. Yet he would not have become an Abraham even had he given away the best he had. What is left out of the Abraham story is the anguish; for to a son the father has the highest and most sacred of obligations. Yet anguish is a dangerous affair for the squeamish, so people forget it. They interchange the words 'Isaac' and 'best'. Everything goes excellently. Should someone in the audience be suffering from insomnia, however, there is likely to be the most appalling misunderstanding. He goes home, he wants to do just like Abraham; for the son is certainly the best thing he has. Should that speaker hear word of this, he might go to the man, and shout: 'Loathsome man, what devil has so possessed you that you wanted to murder your own son?' And this priest, would be surprised at the righteous wrath with which he fulminates against that poor man; he would be pleased with himself, for never had he spoken with such pungency before. If the same speaker still had some slight excess of wit to spare he would surely lose it were the sinner to reply coolly and with dignity: 'It was in fact what you yourself preached on Sunday.'

How could a priest get such an idea into his head? And yet he did so, and the mistake was only that he hadn't known what he was saying.

What explains a contradiction like this speaker's? Is it because whatever Abraham does is great, and if anyone else does the same it is a sin, a crying sin. I have no wish to take part in such mindless praise. If one hasn't the courage to think this thought through, then surely it is better to acquire that courage than to waste time on praise. The ethical expression for what Abraham did is that he was willing to murder Isaac; the religious expression is that he was willing to sacrifice Isaac; but in this contradiction lies the very anguish that can indeed make one sleepless; and yet without that anguish Abraham is not the one he is.

For my own part no thought has frightened me so far. If any should, I hope I will have the honesty to say: 'This thought scares me.' If that is wrong of me I'll no doubt get my punishment. If I had conceded the truth of the judgement that Abraham was a murderer, I am not sure that I would have been able to silence my reverence of him. But if that is what I myself thought, then I would presumably keep quiet, for thoughts like that are not to be intimated to others. However, Abraham does not owe his celebrity to any whim of fate.

Can one speak unreservedly of Abraham, then, without risking that someone will do likewise? Unless I dare to speak quite openly, I will simply keep quiet about Abraham, and not diminish him so that he becomes a snare for the weak.

It should be all right to speak about Abraham. The great can never do harm when grasped in their greatness. It is like a two-edged sword, bringing death and salvation.

I would begin by showing what a devout and God-fearing man Abraham was. Only such a person is subjected to such a trial; but who is such a person? Next I would describe how Abraham loved Isaac. To that end I would make my speech as fervent as is the love of a father for his son. I would hope to describe it in such a way that not many a father in the realm would dare maintain that he loved his son thus. Yet if he did not love as Abraham, all thought of offering Isaac would be a temptation. The result, be that some fathers will simply not want to hear more, but be happy for the time being if they have really succeeded in loving as Abraham did. Should one of them after having caught the greatness and also the appallingness of Abraham's deed, venture out on the road, I would saddle my horse and ride along with him. At every stop before we came to Moriah I would explain to him that he could still turn back, could confess that he lacked the courage, so that if God wanted Isaac God must take him himself.

Having spoken thus, and moved my audience so that they appreciated this dialectical struggle of faith and its gigantic passion, I would not be guilty of the error they might impute to me by thinking: 'Well, he has faith in such a high degree it's enough for us just to hold on to his coat-tails.' For I would add: 'By no means have I faith. I am a shrewd fellow by nature, such as always have great difficulty making the movement of faith. But I wouldn't attach any importance in itself to a difficulty which, by overcoming it, brings a shrewd fellow no further than the most ordinary and simple-minded person has already reached without the difficulty.'

Love, after all, has its priests in the poets; but about faith one hears not a word. Philosophy goes further. Theology sits all painted at the window offering philosophy its delights. It is said to be hard to understand Hegel, while understanding Abraham, why, that's a bagatelle. I believe that I have more or less understood the Hegelian philosophy except in places (I am rash enough to believe) that Hegel himself hasn't been altogether clear. But when I have to think about Abraham I am virtually annihilated. I strain every muscle to catch sight of it, but the same instant I become paralysed.

I am not unfamiliar with the greatness admired in the world, but I cannot fully comprehend Abraham's faith. It presents a paradox that makes me stumble when I reach that height. However, I do not consider faith inferior; on the contrary, I believe it to be the highest. Philosophy should not offer something else in place of faith or belittle it. Philosophy cannot explain faith, but it should understand its own role and offer what it can without diminishing faith's value.

I am aware of life's needs and dangers, and I face them fearlessly. I have encountered horror firsthand, and though I do not possess the courage of faith, I do not cower in fear. However, I acknowledge that my courage cannot be compared to the courage of faith. I cannot blindly trust in the absurd and throw myself into it, as it is impossible for me. I do not boast about this, for I know that faith is of a far higher nature.

I believe that God is love, and this thought brings me indescribable happiness. I yearn for it intensely when it is absent, but I lack the courage of faith. God's love, both directly and inversely, transcends the entirety of reality. I do not whine or complain about this; I neither deny nor hide the fact that faith is something far greater. I can continue to live in my own way and find contentment, but my happiness cannot be compared to the happiness of faith.

I do not burden God with my trivial concerns; I do not dwell on details. I focus solely on my love and keep its pure flame burning. Faith, however, believes that God cares even for the smallest things. In this life, I am content to be wedded to the left hand, while faith humbly demands the right. I acknowledge that this is indeed humility and will never deny it.

I question if my contemporaries can truly make the leap of faith. They pride themselves on doing what they think I'm incapable of—embracing imperfection. I resist speaking of the great in an inhuman manner, as if thousands of years were a vast distance. I prefer to speak of it in human terms, as if it happened yesterday, letting the greatness itself be the measure of elevation or condemnation.

Summoned to a royal procession to the mountain in Moriah, I would not stay at home or delay on the journey. I would arrive promptly, fully prepared. But as I mount the horse, I would think, "Now everything is lost. God demands Isaac. I must sacrifice him, and with him, all my joy. Yet God is love and remains so for me."

In the temporal world, God and I lack a shared language. Some may claim that my immense resignation surpasses Abraham's narrow-mindedness. But it is a falsehood. My immense resignation is a substitute for faith. I could only engage in an infinite movement to find myself and regain composure. I could not love Isaac as Abraham did. While my resolute action may display human courage, truly loving Isaac with all my soul is essential; without it, the affair would be wicked. Yet, I would hesitate at the last moment, though not arriving late at the mountain in Moriah. My behavior would mar the story, for regaining Isaac would leave me at a loss. Finding joy in Isaac, as Abraham did, would be difficult for me. After the infinite movement, proprio motu et propriis auspiciis, I would keep Isaac with pain.

Abraham's actions were precise. He arrived at the mountain neither too early nor too late. He rode the ass down the path, steadfast in his faith. He believed that God would not demand Isaac, yet he was willing to offer him if that was the requirement. Anchored in the absurd, devoid of human calculation, he ascended the mountain. Even as the knife gleamed, he believed that God would spare Isaac. Surprised by the outcome, he embraced a double movement, returning to his original position, and received Isaac with greater joy than before.

But let us go further. Let us imagine that Isaac was actually sacrificed. Abraham had faith, not for future happiness, but for blessed happiness in this world. God had the power to restore Isaac, to resurrect the sacrificial offering. Abraham's faith relied on the absurd, surpassing all human calculations. The sorrow that can drive one to madness is acknowledged, and the strength of will to preserve understanding even when strained is granted. But to lose understanding and the entire finite world it represents, only to regain that same finitude through the absurd, leaves me astounded. Yet I do not diminish its worth; on the contrary, it is a marvel beyond my grasp.

Faith is often misconstrued as crude and vulgar, suitable only for the clumsier souls. However, the truth is quite the opposite. The dialectic of faith is refined and extraordinary, surpassing my comprehension. I can perform grand leaps into infinitude, traversing existence upside down, but the next leap eludes me. I am left in awe of the marvel I cannot achieve. If only Abraham, upon mounting the ass, had said, "Now Isaac is lost. I could have sacrificed him at home instead of embarking on this long journey to Moriah," then I would not require Abraham's presence. Yet, I bow seven times to his name and seventy times to his deed. He did not do as I mentioned, as evidenced by his heartfelt joy upon receiving Isaac. No preparation or adjustment to finitude was necessary. If it were otherwise, Abraham may have loved God, but he would not have had faith. Loving God without faith is self-reflection, whereas loving God with faith is devotion to God.

At this extreme point stands Abraham. The final stage he surpasses is infinite resignation, progressing towards faith. The caricatures of faith, the pitiful lukewarm apathy and the miserable hope, belong to life's wretchedness, scorned by infinite resignation. I cannot comprehend Abraham; all I can do is marvel. If one believes that contemplating the outcome of his story can lead to faith, they deceive themselves and try to cheat God of faith's initial movement, draining the paradox of its life-wisdom. Some may succeed, as our age does not stop at faith's miracle but goes further, turning wine into water.

Would it not be best to remain steadfast in faith? Is it not unsettling that everyone wants to go beyond? When people refuse to stop at love, where are they heading? Towards worldly wisdom, petty calculations, insignificance, and misery, all of which cast doubt upon humanity's divine origin?

Would it not be better to stand firm in faith and take care not to falter? The movement of faith must continuously rely on the strength of the absurd. However, note that one does not lose finitude but gains it entirely. I can describe the movements of faith, but I cannot perform them. It is like hanging in a belt from the ceiling when learning swimming movements; one can describe the motions correctly but is not truly swimming. Similarly, I can describe the movements of faith, but when thrown into the water, although I may appear to be swimming (not among the waders), I make different movements—the movements of infinity. Faith, on the other hand, having performed the movements of infinity, adopts the movements of finitude. Fortunate is the one who can execute those motions, performing a marvel that I will never cease to admire. Whether it is Abraham or a servant, a philosophy professor, or a humble maid, it is inconsequential to me. I focus solely on the movements. However, I genuinely observe those movements and refuse to be fooled by myself or anyone else. The knights of infinite resignation are easily identifiable by their confident and gliding gait. But those who possess the jewel of faith can be deceiving, as their outward appearance bears a striking resemblance to the bourgeois philistine, which both infinite resignation and faith scorn.

In my own experience I have found no reliable examples, though possibly every other person is one. Still, I have tried in vain for several years to track one down. People commonly travel the world over to see rivers and mountains, grotesque breeds of human; they fall into an animal stupor that gapes at existence and they think they have seen something. I am not concerned with this. But if I knew where such a knight of faith lived I would journey to him on foot, for this marvel concerns me absolutely. I would divide my time between looking at him and practising the movements myself, thus devoting all my time to admiring him.

As I said, I haven't found such a one; still, I can very well imagine him. Here he is. The moment I first set eyes on him I jump back and say half aloud: 'Good God! Is this the person, is it really him? He looks just like a tax-gatherer.'

Yet it is him. I cautiously approach, scrutinizing his every gesture and expression, hoping to catch a glimpse of the infinite through some incongruous optical message. Alas, there is none. I examine him thoroughly, searching for any crack through which the infinite might peek. Yet he remains utterly solid. His posture exudes vitality, belonging entirely to the realm of finitude. No well-dressed townsman strolling on a Sunday afternoon could tread the ground with more certainty. He is deeply rooted in the world, no different from any other petit bourgeois. There is nothing peculiar or superior about him, no trace of the strangeness that characterizes the knight of the infinite.

This man takes pleasure in everything, fully engaged in the mundane affairs of life. He attends to his tasks with meticulous attention, as if he were a pen-pusher absorbed in Italian bookkeeping. On Sundays, he takes a holiday and attends church, yet there is no heavenly glimmer or any sign of the incommensurable within him. If one did not know him, it would be impossible to distinguish him from the ordinary crowd. At most, his enthusiastic singing of psalms reveals his robust lungs. In the afternoon, he strolls through the woods, finding delight in everything he encounters—the bustling humanity, the new omnibuses, and the Sound. If you were to meet him on Strandveien, you would think he was a shopkeeper indulging in leisure, such is his way of finding pleasure. He is not a poet, and despite my efforts, I have failed to uncover any secret poetic incommensurability within him.

Towards evening he goes home tirelessly. On the way it occurs to him that his wife will surely have some special little warm dish for his return. If he meets a kindred spirit, he could passionately converse with him about this dish. He firmly believes his wife has that delicacy waiting for him. The sight of him eating it is an enviable one. If his wife doesn't have the dish, curiously enough he is exactly the same. On the road he passes a building-site and talks with another man. He has a building raised in a jiffy, having all that's needed for that. The stranger leaves him thinking: 'That must have been a capitalist,' while my admirable knight thinks: 'Yes, I could surely manage it.' He leisurely looks down on the square where he lives, at everything that goes on - a rat slipping under a board, the children at play - with a composure befitting a sixteen-year-old girl. And yet he is no genius. He smokes his pipe in the evening. He hasn't a worry in the world, and yet he purchases every moment that he lives, 'redeeming the seasonable time' at the dearest price; he does everything on the strength of the absurd. He knows the depths of sorrow, embracing infinite resignation. He has experienced the ecstasy of infinity and the agony of renouncing everything, even the most precious aspects of the world. Yet, to him, the finite holds the same satisfaction as it does for those who have never known anything higher. His embrace of the finite is devoid of anxiety or limitations; it bears no traces of a stunted, fearful existence. He finds security and pleasure in it, as if it were the most certain thing of all. And yet, his earthly form is a testament to the absurd, a new creation borne from its strength.

He infinitely resigned everything, only to reclaim it all through the absurd. He continuously performs the movements of infinity with such precision and grace that he effortlessly derives finitude from them. There is no hint of suspicion that suggests otherwise. Like a skilled dancer leaping into a definitive position without grasping for it, this knight accomplishes what may seem impossible. The majority of people lead disheartened lives, sitting on the sidelines, unwilling to join the dance. The knights of infinity are also dancers, possessing elevation. They ascend and descend, a joyous spectacle to behold. However, when they descend, they cannot immediately assume a stable position. There is a moment of wavering, revealing their inherent foreignness to the world. The degree of their skill may determine the extent of this wavering, but even the most skilled cannot conceal it. One can recognize them not when they soar through the air, but when they land on the ground. Their ability to land and seamlessly transition into walking, transforming the leap of life into a pedestrian stride, expressing the sublime in the ordinary – that is a feat reserved solely for the knight of faith. It is a marvel beyond compare.

In a specific case, a young man falls deeply in love with a princess, making this love the essence of his entire existence. However, the realization of this love in reality seems impossible. The miserable slaves of despair dismiss such love as foolishness, suggesting more practical matches. But the knight of infinite resignation does not renounce his love, not for any worldly glory. He is no trifler. Before fully embracing the love, he ensures that it genuinely defines his life. His soul is too proud and healthy to waste anything on trivial pursuits. Fearlessly, he allows the love to infiltrate his innermost thoughts, entwining itself in every aspect of his consciousness. If the love turns into sorrow, he will be unable to detach himself from it. The exhilaration of feeling it course through his every nerve is matched by the solemnity of one who has consumed a cup of poison, sensing its effects in every drop of blood. This moment is both life and death.

Having immersed himself completely in love, he is undeterred by the impossibilities that life presents. He contemplates his life circumstances, summons his swift and obedient thoughts, guiding them with his wand as they scatter in various directions. However, when they return as messengers of sorrow, confirming the impossibility, he remains calm. He dismisses them, opting for solitude, and performs the movement. The significance of my words lies in the proper execution of this movement. First and foremost, the knight must possess the strength to concentrate his entire life's purpose and the essence of reality into a single wish. Without this focused concentration, his soul would disintegrate from the outset, rendering him incapable of making the movement. Instead, he would navigate life cautiously, akin to capitalists who distribute their investments across multiple securities to mitigate losses and gain profits. In short, he would not embody the essence of a true knight.

Secondly, the knight's strength lies in consolidating the result of his reflections into a single act of consciousness. Without this focus, his soul disintegrates, forever occupied with mundane tasks, unable to enter the eternal realm.

So the knight makes the movement, but what movement is it? Does he seek to forget? No! The knight does not contradict himself; it is contradictory to forget one's entire life's content and remain unchanged. He has no desire to become someone else. Only lower natures forget themselves and transform. Deeper natures never forget themselves or become something other than what they were.

Thus, the knight remembers everything. Memory itself is the pain, and yet in his infinite resignation, he reconciles with existence. His love for the princess takes on the form of eternal love, acquiring a religious character. It is transfigured into a love for the eternal being, which, though unfulfilled, still grants him reconciliation through the eternal consciousness of the validity of his love in a form that no reality can strip away.

Fools and young people believe that everything is possible for a human being, but that is a grave mistake. Spiritually, everything is possible, but in the finite world, many things are not. The knight, however, makes the impossible possible by expressing it spiritually, renouncing it. The desire that once aimed to manifest in reality but faced impossibility now turns inward, yet it is not lost or forgotten. Sometimes, the desire's unconscious workings awaken the memory, while at other times, the knight himself awakens it. He is too proud to let the entirety of his life's content appear as a fleeting affair. He keeps this love young, and it grows with him in years and beauty. He doesn't require a specific occasion for his love to grow. The princess is lost to him from the moment he made the movement. He doesn't need the sensual stimulation or the constant farewells of finite encounters. His memory of her is eternal, unlike those lovers who quickly forget each other. He understands that one should be self-sufficient even in loving another. He pays no finite attention to the princess's actions, proving his infinite resignation. If she shares the same disposition, their love will develop beautifully. They will belong to the same eternal order of knighthood, transcending gender distinctions. Both will keep their love vibrant and overcome their agony. Although they may not physically unite, their connection will be harmoniously pre-established. If a moment were to arise where their love could manifest in time, they would pick up right where they left off, as if they had been united from the beginning.

The one who understands this, whether man or woman, cannot be deceived. Lower natures are the ones who fall for deception. True love is unknown to those who lack this pride, but those who possess it cannot be fooled by the world's tricks and cunning. In infinite resignation, there is peace, repose, and a pain that reconciles one to existence. Infinite resignation is that shirt in the old fable. The thread is spun with tears, bleached by tears, the shirt sewn in tears, but then it also gives better protection than iron and steel. A defect of the fable is that a third party is able to make the material. The one who understands this, whether man or woman, cannot be deceived. Lower natures are the ones who fall for deception. True love is unknown to those who lack this pride, but those who possess it cannot be fooled by the world's tricks and cunning. In infinite resignation, there is peace, repose, and a reconciling pain.

Infinite resignation is the penultimate stage before faith. Without making this movement, one cannot have faith. It is through infinite resignation that the eternal validity of one's existence becomes clear, allowing the grasp of existence through faith.

Now, let us introduce the knight of faith in the discussed case. He follows the same path as the other knight, renouncing the love that defines his life and finding reconciliation in pain. But here comes the marvel: he takes one more extraordinary step. He declares, "Nevertheless, I believe that I shall attain her, based on the absurd, on the fact that all things are possible for God." The absurd is not a mere intellectual concept like improbability or unexpectedness. When the knight resigned, he understood the impossibility of attaining his desire from a human standpoint. It was a conclusion of the understanding, and he had the mental clarity to reach it. However, in an infinite sense, the possibility remained through renouncing it as a finite possibility. Accepting this paradox is simultaneously giving it up. Yet, for the understanding, there is no contradiction in holding onto it, as understanding operates solely within the finite world where it remains impossible. The knight of faith comprehends this just as clearly. The only thing that can save him is the absurd, and he apprehends it through faith. He acknowledges the impossibility while simultaneously believing in the absurd. If he were to claim faith without recognizing the impossibility with utmost passion and conviction, he would deceive himself, and his testimony would hold no weight, as he would not have even reached the stage of infinite resignation.

Faith is not an aesthetic emotion; it surpasses that level because it necessitates resignation. It is not an immediate inclination of the heart, but rather the paradox of existence. Thus, the certainty of a young girl that her desire will be fulfilled, despite all difficulties, does not equate to faith, even if she has been raised by Christian parents and attended church for a year. Her conviction, rooted in childlike simplicity and innocence, elevates her character and gives her an otherworldly dimension. She can work wonders, captivating the finite powers of existence and even moving stones to tears. However, in her distraction, she may appeal to Herod as easily as she would to Pilate, attempting to persuade the whole world through her pleas. Her certainty is endearing, and there is much to learn from her. Yet, it does not teach us how to make the proper movements. Her certainty does not dare to confront the impossibility in the anguish of resignation.

Faith is not merely an aesthetic emotion; it surpasses that level because it necessitates resignation. It is not the immediate inclination of the heart, but rather the paradox of existence. Therefore, the certainty of a young girl, despite difficulties, that her desire will be fulfilled does not equate to faith. Even if she has been raised by Christian parents and attended church, her conviction stems from childlike simplicity and innocence. While her assurance ennobles her nature and grants her a preternatural dimension, enabling her to charm existence's finite powers and evoke tears from stones, it does not teach the art of making movements. Her certainty does not face impossibility head-on in the pain of resignation.

I understand that it requires strength, energy, and spiritual freedom to make the infinite movement of resignation. I acknowledge that it can be done, but the next step baffles me; it leaves my mind reeling. To resign and then, based on the absurd, to obtain everything, to attain desires whole and complete—such a feat demands superhuman powers; it is truly a marvel. However, I can perceive that the conviction of the young girl pales in comparison to an unshakable faith that persists even in the face of impossibility. Whenever I contemplate making this movement, dizziness overtakes me. I simultaneously admire it immensely, yet immense anxiety grips my soul, for what is it to test God? Nonetheless, this movement remains an act of faith, regardless of how philosophy, in its attempt to blur concepts, may try to pass it off as faith, or how theology may attempt to sell it cheaply.

Resignation does not require faith, as it grants me my eternal consciousness—a purely philosophical movement that I undertake when necessary and can discipline myself to perform. Every time something finite surpasses me, I starve myself until I make the movement. For me, my eternal consciousness, which is my love for God, is higher than anything. Resignation does not demand faith, but faith is necessary to obtain even the slightest bit more than my eternal consciousness, for that "more" is the paradox. The movements are often confused. It is said that faith is needed to renounce everything, and strangely, people complain about losing faith, yet when we assess their progress, we find that they have not advanced beyond the point where they should be making the infinite movement of resignation.

Through resignation, I renounce everything—an act I undertake alone. When I fail to make this movement, it is due to my own cowardice, weakness, lack of enthusiasm, and failure to grasp the significance of the profound dignity afforded to every human being—to be one's own censor, a dignity far greater than being the Censor General of the entire Roman Republic. This movement is a personal endeavor, and what I gain is my eternal consciousness, a blessed alignment with my love for the eternal being. On the other hand, through faith, I do not renounce anything; rather, I receive everything. It is said that someone with faith like a mustard seed can move mountains. It takes sheer human courage to renounce all of temporality to attain eternity, and once won, I cannot renounce it for all eternity, as that would contradict itself. However, it takes paradoxical and humble courage to embrace the entirety of temporality based on the absurd, and that is the courage of faith.

By faith, Abraham did not renounce his claim on Isaac; rather, he received Isaac through his faith. The rich young man, through his act of resignation, should have given away everything. However, the knight of faith would say to him, "Believe that, on the strength of the absurd, you shall get every penny back." These words should not be taken lightly by the once wealthy young man, as his resignation would be in a sorry state if he gave away his possessions out of boredom.

It all comes down to temporality and finitude. I can, by my own strength, renounce everything and find peace and repose in the pain. I can endure anything, even if madness itself were to confront me, urging me to wear the fool's costume. As long as my love for God triumphs over my worldly happiness, I can still save my soul. In that final moment, I can concentrate my entire being on a single glance towards the heaven from which all good gifts come. This glance signifies my fidelity to my love. Then, calmly, I can put on the costume. Without this romanticism, one has sold their soul, regardless of whether they received a kingdom or a meager piece of silver. But, with my own strength, I cannot attain even the slightest thing pertaining to finitude. I constantly expend my energy renouncing everything. I can relinquish the princess without sulking and find joy, peace, and repose in my pain. However, I cannot regain her through my own strength since that strength is precisely what I employ to renounce my claim. But by faith, proclaims the marvelous knight, you will attain her through the power of the absurd.

Alas, I am incapable of making this movement! Each time I attempt to initiate it, everything spins around, and I retreat back to the pain of resignation. I can swim in life, but I am too heavy for this mysterious floating. I cannot exist in such a way that my opposition to existence manifests itself as the most beautiful and secure harmony in every instant. Yet, it must be glorious to obtain the princess—I affirm this constantly. The knight of resignation, who fails to express such affirmation, is a deceiver. He has not cherished a single desire, nor has he preserved his desire's youthfulness within its pain. Some may find it convenient that the desire is no longer alive and that the sting of pain has dulled. But such individuals are not knights. A free-born soul, if it catches itself in such a state, would despise itself, start anew, and, above all, refuse to be deceived in its soul. And yet, it must be wonderful to attain the princess. Only the knight of faith is truly happy; he alone is the heir to the finite, while the knight of resignation remains a stranger, a foreigner.

To obtain the princess in this manner, to live joyfully and happily in her company every day, we must acknowledge that the knight of resignation may also acquire the princess, even though he has recognized the impossibility of their future happiness. Living joyfully and happily in this manner, every moment on the strength of the absurd, entails seeing the sword constantly hanging over the loved one's head. Yet, instead of finding repose in the pain of resignation, one discovers joy through the power of the absurd. That is truly remarkable. The one who accomplishes this is great—the only great one. The thought of it stirs my soul, which has never been stingy in its admiration of greatness.

If everyone in my generation, who refuses to settle for faith, truly understands life's horror and comprehends the meaning of Daub's soldier standing guard alone with a loaded gun by a powder magazine on a stormy night, experiencing strange thoughts; if those unwilling to stop at faith possess the strength of soul to acknowledge the impossibility of their desires and have reconciled themselves through pain; if they have also achieved the remarkable feat of embracing the entirety of existence on the strength of the absurd, then what I am writing here is a speech praising my generation, delivered by the least significant among them, the one who can only make the movement of resignation. However, I cannot grasp why they refuse to stop at faith or why some are embarrassed to admit they have faith. That eludes my understanding. If I ever manage to make this leap, I would drive forward with great determination.

Could it be that all the bourgeois philistinism I witness in life, which I only condemn through my actions and not my words, is not what it appears to be? Is it truly a marvel? It is conceivable, considering that our hero of faith bore a striking resemblance to it, transcending even irony and humor. Much is said about irony and humor in our time, especially by those who have never truly practiced them but claim to understand everything. I am not entirely unfamiliar with these two passions; my knowledge extends beyond what German and German Danish compendia offer. I am aware that irony and humor reflect upon themselves, belonging to the realm of infinite resignation, drawing strength from the individual's incomparability with reality.

The final movement, the paradoxical movement of faith, eludes me. Whether it is a duty or not, I would be more than willing to

perform it. Whether one has the right to say so is a matter between the individual and the eternal being who is the object of faith, a matter that can only be resolved through a peaceful agreement. However, what everyone can do is embrace the infinite movement of resignation, and I would consider anyone who believes they cannot to be a coward. Faith, on the other hand, is a different story. Yet, no one has the right to mislead others into thinking that faith is inferior or easy when, in fact, it is the greatest and most challenging pursuit of all.

Some interpret the story of Abraham differently, praising God's mercy for giving him Isaac once again, as if it were just a trial. But they conveniently overlook the details. They imagine a swift journey on a winged horse, instantly arriving on Mount Moriah and seeing the ram. They forget that Abraham traveled on an ass, taking three days to reach his destination, needing time to chop wood, bind Isaac, and sharpen the knife.

Yet, they praise Abraham as if it were all effortless. The speaker and the listener pass through it smoothly, without any trouble. It's as if they are saying, "Wait a minute, and you'll see the ram, trial over." It's as if there were no need for patience or struggle. If someone dares to question this ease, the speaker, in all his self-righteousness, would condemn them, claiming that life is just a trial.

Let us either forget about Abraham altogether or be horrified by the paradoxical significance of his life. Only then can we understand that our time, like any other, can find joy in faith. If Abraham is not a mere decoration or a triviality, then the fault lies not in the sinner's desire to emulate him, but in the failure to recognize the greatness of Abraham's deed. Each person must judge for themselves if they have the inclination and courage to undergo such a trial. The speaker's contradictory behavior diminishes Abraham's importance while denying others the right to follow suit.

Should we not dare to speak of Abraham? I believe we should. If I were to discuss him, I would first portray the pain of the trial. I would emphasize the fear, distress, and torment experienced by the father, in order to truly convey the extent of Abraham's suffering while maintaining his faith. I would remind people that the journey lasted three and a half days, far longer than the two thousand years that separate us from Abraham. I would also stress that everyone has the right to change their mind before embarking on such a path, and that it is possible to retract and turn back at any moment. By doing so, I see no danger, and I am not afraid of inspiring a desire in people to be tested like Abraham. However, attempting to cheapen the significance of Abraham's story while discouraging others from following in his footsteps is simply laughable.

I aim to extract the dialectical element from Abraham's story, revealing the monstrous paradox of faith. It transforms murder into a holy act, pleasing to God, returning Isaac to Abraham. This paradox lies beyond comprehension, as faith surpasses thinking's limits.

Problema I: Is There a Teleological Suspension of the Ethical?

The ethical is universal and applies at every moment. It exists within itself, independent of external factors, and serves as the ultimate purpose for everything outside of it. When an individual aligns themselves with the universal, they fulfill their ethical duty. They must relinquish their particularity to become one with the universal. However, should the individual attempt to assert their particularity in opposition to the universal, they commit a sin. Only by recognizing this transgression can they reconcile themselves with the universal.

When the individual, having embraced the universal, experiences the temptation to assert their particularity, they find themselves in a precarious state. To overcome this temptation, they must surrender their individuality to the universal through repentance. In this perspective, the highest state of being, the ethical life, and eternal blessedness merge as one. Suspending the teleological purpose would contradict its preservation in a higher realm.

Hegel correctly identifies the ethical life as surpassing the perspective of the single individual, deeming it a "moral form of evil" that must be transcended within the teleology of ethical existence. To remain at this stage indicates either sin or a state of temptation. However, Hegel's mistake lies in his treatment of faith. He fails to voice a clear protest against the exalted status bestowed upon Abraham as the father of faith, instead suggesting he should be condemned as a murderer.

Faith embodies a profound paradox: the single individual rises above the universal while simultaneously being part of it. If faith were non-existent, then Abraham's faith would lose its meaning, even though faith has always been present. If the ethical life encompasses all aspects of existence and leaves no room for the incommensurable, except for what is deemed evil, then additional categories beyond those of the Greek philosophers would be unnecessary. Hegel, with his knowledge of Greek philosophy, should have addressed this omission.

In summary, the ethical's universality demands the individual's alignment with the universal while surrendering their particularity. Hegel correctly critiques the limitations of the single individual but falls short in his treatment of faith. Faith embodies a paradox where the individual surpasses the universal, and if faith is disregarded, the significance of Abraham's faith is diminished. The ethical life, if all-encompassing, renders extra categories unnecessary. Hegel's oversight in these matters should have been addressed.

One often hears people resort to clichés, claiming that Christianity is a beacon of light while paganism dwells in darkness. Such statements strike me as peculiar since deep thinkers and serious artists still seek inspiration from the eternal youth of the Greeks. Perhaps these individuals don't know what to say but feel compelled to say something. It's easy to dismiss paganism as lacking faith, but without a clear understanding of faith, such assertions become clichés. As Boileau astutely noted, "a fool can always find a greater fool who admires him."

Faith embodies a paradox: the individual, as a particular, surpasses the universal and is justified before it. This superiority is not subordination but an absolute relation to the absolute. This paradox remains inaccessible to thought and defies mediation. And yet, faith exists within this paradox. Alternatively, one can argue that faith has never truly existed precisely because it has always existed. This poses a challenge to Abraham's story.

Many individuals might mistake this paradox for temptation, but that should not silence its discussion. While some may naturally have an aversion to the paradox, that is no reason to redefine faith so that everyone can possess it. Those who possess faith should be able to provide criteria for distinguishing the paradox from temptation.

The story of Abraham exemplifies a teleological suspension of the ethical. Scholars have sought analogies to this story, but their attempts to equate it with other narratives fall short. Abraham represents faith, and his life is not just paradoxical, but so incomprehensible that it defies thought. Acting on the strength of the absurd, he demonstrates that as an individual, he transcends the universal. This paradox is unmediated, and any attempt at mediation would expose Abraham to temptation. Yet, through the absurd, he regains Isaac. Abraham is not a tragic hero but something entirely different—a murderer or a man of faith. He lacks the middle-term that saves tragic heroes. Although I admire Abraham in a somewhat lunatic sense, I struggle to fully comprehend him.

In conclusion, clichéd comparisons between Christianity and paganism oversimplify the complexity of faith. Faith resides within a paradox, defying explanation and eluding thought. The story of Abraham encapsulates this paradox, challenging conventional notions of heroism. Abraham's actions defy rationality, making him an enigmatic figure deserving both admiration and confusion.

Abraham's ethical duty as a father is to love his son more than himself. Yet, within the ethical realm, there are various levels of duty. Let us explore whether this story contains a higher expression of ethics that justifies his actions without surpassing the ethical's own teleology.

In a situation where a national undertaking is halted by divine displeasure, when a dead calm mocks all efforts, and a seer reveals that a young girl must be sacrificed, the father must exhibit heroism. He must hide his grief and bear the burden of a king, even as his heart breaks. The pain, initially shared with only a few confidants, will become known to the entire population. They will witness his sacrifice for the greater good, offering his beloved daughter, a beautiful maiden, for the well-being of all. The daughter's tears will touch him, and the father will turn away his face, yet the hero will raise the knife. The news will reach the ancestral home, causing maidens across Greece to blush with admiration. Even the daughter's betrothed, if she were a bride, would not be angry but proud to have been part of the father's act, as she belonged to him more tenderly than to her father.

When Jephthah, the courageous judge who saved Israel, binds himself and God with a promise, he must transform his beloved daughter's joy into sorrow. All of Israel will grieve with the young maiden, but every free-born person will understand and admire Jephthah. Every strong-hearted woman will hold him in high regard, and every maiden in Israel will aspire to be like his daughter. For what good is triumph if Jephthah makes a promise but fails to keep it? The victory would once again be lost to the people.

When a son forgets his duty and the State entrusts the father with the sword of justice, the father must display heroism by forgetting that the guilty one is his own flesh and blood. He will nobly conceal his pain, and the nation, including the son, will admire him. Every interpretation of Rome's laws will recall that many may have understood them more learnedly, but none more gloriously than Brutus.

On the other hand, if Agamemnon had sent for Iphigenia while his fleet sailed smoothly, or if Jephthah had told his daughter without any binding promise, "Mourn now for two months, for I shall sacrifice you," or if Brutus had a righteous son and still commanded his executioners— who would understand them? If, when asked why they did it, these three replied, "It is a trial in which we are being tested," would that explanation be more comprehensible?

When Agamemnon, Jephthah, and Brutus heroically bear their pain, willingly sacrifice their loved ones, and have only the outward act remaining, noble souls around the world shed tears of sympathy and admiration. But if, at that crucial moment, they added the words, "It won't happen," who would understand them? If they further explained, "We believe it based on the absurd," who would comprehend them better? For who would not acknowledge the absurdity? Yet, who would understand that belief can arise from that very absurdity?

The difference between the tragic hero and Abraham is obvious enough. The tragic hero stays within the ethical. He lets an expression of the ethical have its telos in a higher expression of the ethical; he reduces the ethical relation between father and son, or daughter and father, to a sentiment that has its dialectic in its relation to the idea of the ethical life. Here, then, there can be no question of a teleological suspension of the ethical itself.

Abraham's actions surpass the ethical realm and are driven by a higher purpose beyond it. There is no way to reconcile Abraham's action with the universal other than acknowledging that he goes against it. His act has no connection to saving a nation, upholding the state, or appeasing gods. If anyone was angry, it could only be the deity directed at Abraham, and his action remains entirely personal. The ethical life, as understood in the universal sense, does not apply here. If there was any universality present, it lay latent in Isaac, who would cry out, "Don't do it, you are destroying everything."

So why does Abraham proceed? For God's sake, which is synonymous with doing it for his own sake. He does it for God's sake because God demands this test of his faith, and he does it for his own sake to be able to provide the proof. The unity lies in the notion of temptation or trial. But what does that mean? Typically, temptation prevents someone from fulfilling a duty, yet here the ethical itself becomes the temptation that hinders Abraham from carrying out God's will. And what is the duty? It precisely represents God's will.

Understanding Abraham requires a new category. Paganism does not encompass such a relationship with the divine. The tragic hero does not engage in a private connection with God; instead, the ethical itself is divine, allowing for the reconciliation of paradox through the universal.

Abraham cannot be reconciled or speak in a mediated manner. The moment he speaks, he expresses the universal, and without it, no one can comprehend him. Therefore, when Abraham attempts to express himself universally, he must refer to his situation as one of temptation because he lacks a higher expression of the universal that surpasses the universal he transgresses.

While Abraham evokes admiration, he also instills horror. The person who sacrifices the finite for the infinite, motivated by duty, is secure. The tragic hero abandons certainty for something even more certain, and observers can confidently behold him. But what does one make of the person who gives up the universal for something beyond the universal? Can it be anything other than temptation? If it is not temptation and the individual has misunderstood, what salvation is there for him? He endures the pain of the tragic hero, negates all worldly joy, abandons everything, and perhaps, in the same instant, deprives himself of the exalted joy he cherishes so dearly. Observers cannot understand such a person or confidently look upon him. Perhaps the believer's intention is impossible; it may be unthinkable. And if it is possible, but the individual has misunderstood the deity, what salvation awaits him?

The tragic hero elicits tears, and they are rightfully shed. Who among us did not weep alongside Agamemnon? But who could dare weep for Abraham? Abraham evokes a religious horror, similar to Israel's encounter with Mount Sinai. What if the solitary man ascending Mount Moriah, whose peak soars above the plains of Aulis, is not a sleepwalker confidently treading over the abyss? What if someone standing at the foot of the mountain, witnessing his ascent, trembles with anxiety and cannot even shout out of respect and fear, fearing that the man may be distracted or mistaken? Thanks and thanks again to anyone who extends a leaf of words to shield the nakedness of one assaulted by life's sorrows. Thanks to you, great Shakespeare, who can express everything exactly as it is. Yet, why did you never give voice to this torment? Was it a secret you kept, like the name of a beloved that one cannot bear to mention? A poet purchases the power to utter the grim secrets of others at the cost of a secret they themselves cannot speak. A poet is not an apostle; they can only cast out devils using the power of the devil.

When the ethical is suspended in a teleological sense, how does the individual who embodies this suspension exist? They exist as the particular in opposition to the universal. Does this mean they sin? From an ideal perspective, this form resembles sin, just as a child's unconsciousness of its own existence does not negate the fact that, ideally, its existence is sinful and that the ethical imposes its demands on the child at every moment. If this form cannot be seen as anything other than sin, then judgement has been passed on Abraham. How did Abraham exist? He had faith. This paradox keeps him at the extreme, incomprehensible to others. The paradox lies in his absolute relation to the absolute as the single individual. Is he justified? Once again, the justification is the paradox itself, for if he embodies the paradox, it is not because he represents anything universal but because he is the particular.

How does the individual assure themselves of their justification? It is easy to reduce existence to the idea of the State or a concept of society. By doing so, one can mediate, avoiding the paradox of the single individual being higher than the universal. This can be pointed out by a proposition from Pythagoras, stating that odd numbers are more perfect than even numbers. If an answer is given in the direction of the paradox in our time, it might go like this: "That's to be judged by the outcome." A hero who becomes the scandal of their generation, aware of their incomprehensible paradox, fearlessly cries out to their contemporaries, "The future will show I was right!" Such cries are rare today, as our age fails to produce heroes but benefits from having fewer caricatures. Whenever we hear the words "That's to be judged by the outcome," we immediately know whom we are conversing with. Those who speak this way form a populous tribe that I shall call the "lecturers." They live in their thoughts, secure in their lives, holding permanent positions with promising prospects in a well-organized State. They are distanced by centuries, even millennia, from the upheavals of existence, with no fear that such things could occur again. What would the police and newspapers say? Their purpose is to judge the great, to judge them based on the outcome. This conduct towards greatness reveals a curious blend of arrogance and pitifulness. Arrogance because they feel entitled to pass judgement, pitifulness because they see no connection between their lives and those of the great. Anyone with a trace of nobility of mind cannot become so cold and detached as to disregard, when approaching the great, the fact that since the beginning of Creation, the outcome comes last. To truly learn from the great, one must focus on the beginning. If someone on the verge of action were to judge themselves solely by the outcome, they would never begin. Even if the result brings joy to the world, it cannot aid the hero. The hero only knows the result when everything is over, but they become a hero by virtue of beginning.

However, the outcome, in its dialectic nature as finitude's response to the infinite question, is incompatible with the existence of the hero. Should we assume that Abraham's justification for relating himself as the single individual to the universal lies in the fact that he miraculously received Isaac? If Abraham had actually sacrificed Isaac, would that have made him any less justified?

But it is the outcome that piques our curiosity, akin to reaching the end of a book; we desire none of the fear, distress, or paradox. We flirt with the outcome aesthetically, as it arrives unexpectedly and effortlessly, like a prize in a lottery. Upon hearing the outcome, we feel improved. Yet, no temple robber toiling in chains is as despicable as the one who pillages the sacred in this manner. Not even Judas, who sold his master for thirty pieces of silver, is more contemptible than someone who would sell greatness in such a manner.

It goes against my nature to speak inhumanly of greatness, to let its magnificence blur into an indistinct outline from a distance or to portray it as great without the human element that defines its greatness. For it is not what happens to me that makes me great, but what I do. Surely, no one believes that someone becomes great simply by winning the grand lottery prize. Even for a person born in humble circumstances, I expect them to be humane enough to

envision the king's castle not just from afar, through vague dreams of grandeur, but to approach it with confidence and dignity. They should not be so inhuman as to violate every rule of respect by barging into the king's salon straight from the street. By doing so, they lose more than the king. Instead, they should take pleasure in observing every rule of decorum with joyful enthusiasm, which will make them genuine and open-hearted. This analogy is imperfect, for the spiritual distance is far greater. I implore everyone not to think so inhumanely of themselves as to hesitate to set foot in the palaces where not only the memory of the chosen resides but the chosen themselves. They should not shamelessly thrust their kinship upon them but feel elation each time they bow before them. They should be candid, confident, and something more than a mere cleaning woman, for unless they aspire to be more, they will never enter those places.

What will truly aid them are the fear and distress that test the great, for otherwise, if they have a drop of red blood in them, they will only provoke righteous envy. Anything that can only be great from a distance, anything that people attempt to exalt with empty and hollow phrases, is reduced to insignificance by their own actions.

Was there ever anyone in the world as great as the blessed woman, the Virgin Mary, the mother of God? Yet, how do people speak of her? Describing her as favored among women does not make her great. If not for the strange fact that those who listen can think as inhumanly as those who speak, every young girl would surely ask, "Why am I not favored too?" And if I had nothing more to say, I would not dismiss such a question as foolish. In regards to favors, abstractly speaking, everyone is equally entitled. What is left out are the distress, fear, and paradox.

My thoughts are as pure as the next person's, and surely anyone capable of thinking in this manner will have pure thoughts as well. If not, something dreadful awaits them. Once these images come to mind, they cannot be easily dispelled, and if one sins against them, their quiet wrath, more terrifying than the clamor of ten voracious critics, will exact dreadful vengeance. Mary indeed bore the child miraculously, but it happened to her "after the manner of women," a time filled with fear, distress, and paradox. The angel, though a ministering spirit, did not visit all the young girls in Israel and explain Mary's extraordinary situation. He came only to Mary, and no one could understand her. Yet, what woman endured greater indignity than Mary? Isn't it true that those whom God blesses, He damns in the same breath? This is the spirit's understanding of Mary, and she is not, as offensive as it is to say, the fine lady adorned in luxury playing with a divine child. Nevertheless, by declaring, "Behold the handmaid of the Lord," she is great. It should not be difficult to explain why she became the mother of God. She requires no worldly admiration, just as Abraham needs no tears. Neither was a hero or heroine, but both became greater because of the distress, agony, and paradox, not by being relieved of them.

It is truly remarkable when a poet presents a tragic hero for public admiration and boldly says, "Weep for him, for he deserves it." There is greatness in earning the tears of those who deserve to shed them. It is even greater when the poet dares to hold the crowd accountable, urging them to examine their own worthiness to weep for the hero, as the lamentations of sniveling cowards demean the sacred. But greater than all of this is when the knight of faith dares to say to the noble person who would weep for him, "Do not weep for me, but weep for yourself."

We are stirred, longing for those beautiful times, desiring to see Christ walking in the promised land. We forget the fear, distress, and paradox. Was it so easy not to be mistaken? Wasn't it a fearful thought that the man walking among us was God? Wasn't it terrifying to share a meal with him? Was it so simple to become an apostle? Yet, the passage of eighteen centuries helps us. It aids the shabby deception in which we deceive ourselves and others. I do not possess the courage to wish to be contemporaneous with such events, but for that reason, I do not harshly judge those who were mistaken, nor do I think less of those who recognized the truth.

Now, I return to Abraham. In the time before the outcome, either

Abraham was a murderer every minute, or we embrace the paradox that surpasses all mediation. So Abraham's story contains a teleological suspension of the ethical. This one man has become higher than the universal. This paradox cannot be mediated. If this is not the case with Abraham, then he is not a tragic hero but a murderer. A tragic hero can become a human being by his own strength, but not the knight of faith. Many can lend advice to someone on the tragic hero's hard path; but he who walks the path of faith no one can advise or even understand. Faith is a marvel, and yet no human being is excluded from it; for that in which all human life is united is passion, and faith is a passion.

Problema II: Is There an Absolute Duty to God?

In the ethical perspective, the universal is synonymous with the ethical, and therefore, all duty is ultimately duty to God. However, when we speak of duty to God, we do not establish a direct relationship with God within the duty itself. The duty becomes duty to God by being referred to God, but our engagement is primarily with the neighbor whom we are called to love. It is worth noting that if we love God in this particular sense, it becomes a tautology since God is understood in an abstract sense as the divine or the universal, which is synonymous with duty. Thus, the entirety of human existence becomes self-contained within this sphere of the ethical, where God becomes an invisible point, a mere thought, and his power is found only within the ethical realm that encompasses all aspects of existence.

If one were to attempt to love God in a different sense than previously mentioned, it would be an extravagant endeavor, as one would be infatuated with a phantom. Such a phantom, if it had the strength to express itself, would dismiss the misguided love, saying, "Stay where you belong, for I do not ask for your love." Therefore, any attempt to love God outside the prescribed understanding is futile and without foundation. The love referred to by Rousseau, for example, where a person loves the Kaffirs instead of their neighbor, would be considered suspicious in the same way.

While this perspective may seem coherent and all-encompassing, it negates the existence of an incomparable aspect within human life. According to this viewpoint, any incommensurability would be the result of chance or randomness that does not have any significant implications when existence is examined from the perspective of the Idea. This is where Hegel's philosophy aligns, as it considers faith and even regards Abraham as its father. However, this interpretation of faith overlooks the unique paradox it embodies. Faith introduces an interiority that transcends and cannot be reconciled with exteriority. It is crucial to highlight that this new interiority is not identical to the initial interiority found in childhood. Recent philosophy has made the hasty substitution of the immediate for faith, thereby reducing faith to a mere feeling, mood, or idiosyncrasy. Although philosophy rightly argues against this reduction, it lacks sufficient grounds for making such assertions.

Faith emerges after a movement of infinity, characterized by an encounter with the absurd. Prior to faith, there is a profound sense of the infinite, and it is within this context that faith unexpectedly arises. It is possible to comprehend this movement of faith without claiming to possess faith itself. If faith were nothing more than what philosophy reduces it to, then even Socrates surpassed this understanding through his intellectual exploration. Socrates, in his pursuit of wisdom, embraced the movement of the infinite as he expressed his infinite resignation through his recognition of his own ignorance. This task of engaging with the infinite is a formidable challenge, even though it may be scorned in contemporary times. Only when the individual has fully immersed themselves in the infinite, exhausting their capacity, can faith truly emerge.

In summary, the ethical view encompasses duty to God within the universal, but it lacks a direct relationship with God in the fulfillment of duties. Attempts to love God outside the prescribed understanding are futile. Hegel's philosophy, which prioritizes the external over the internal, fails to fully comprehend the paradox of faith. Faith introduces a unique interiority that cannot be reconciled with exteriority. Recent philosophy's substitution of the immediate for faith is misguided. Prior to faith, there is a movement of infinity, and faith emerges unexpectedly through encounters with the absurd. Socrates, through his pursuit of wisdom, demonstrated an understanding of the movement of the infinite. Faith only emerges when one has fully engaged with the infinite, surpassing their own limitations.

Then faith's paradox is that the single individual is higher than the universal. The single individual determines his relation to the universal through his relation to the absolute, not vice-versa. There is an absolute duty to God; the individual relates himself absolutely to this obligation, as the single individual to the absolute. The duty to love God is in a very different sense; for if this duty is absolute the ethical is reduced to the relative. But the ethical is not done away with; rather, it gets a different expression, the paradoxical expression, so that, e.g., love of God can cause the knight of faith to give his love of his neighbour the opposite expression to that which is his duty ethically speaking.

In the paradox of faith, there is no room for mediation or explanation. The individual who embodies faith stands alone, unable to be understood or communicated with by others. Even if one were to attempt to explain their actions, it would be futile, as faith transcends universal categories and operates in the realm of the single individual.

Abraham's story exemplifies this paradox. Ethically, he should love his son Isaac, but his absolute duty to God takes precedence. Abraham's response to the question why is that it is a trial and temptation, but it is not a satisfying answer. The paradox lies in the simultaneous expression of extreme egoism and absolute devotion.

Partnership or understanding between individuals in this realm is impossible. Each individual must embrace the paradox themselves to become a knight of faith. Even if one seeks to take responsibility for faith through another, they can never truly attain it. Only the single individual, facing the terror and greatness of faith, can fully comprehend it.

Attempting to reconcile the sacrifice of Isaac under universal terms is absurd, as the single individual exists outside of the universal. Any explanation can only be grasped by the individual themselves, and they can never be assured of others' understanding. This highlights the solitude and personal nature of faith, where the single individual embraces the paradox without relying on external validation. Ultimately, faith defies explanation and cannot be mediated into universal concepts. It exists as a paradox, confounding conventional ethical norms and challenging the understanding of others.

Luke 14.26 presents a remarkable teaching on the absolute duty to God. Who can bear to hear it? And for that reason it is heard very seldom. Yet this silence is only a futile evasion. These words occur in the New Testament, and finds the information that misein [to hate], both here and in some other passages, is used per meiosin [by adopting a weaker sense] to mean: minus diligo [love less], posthabeo [give less priority to], non colo [show no respect to], nihil facio [make nothing of].

The context in which these words occur does not corroborate this tasteful explanation. For in the next verses there is a story about someone who plans to erect a tower but first estimates his capacity to do so, to prevent public ridicule later. The link between this story and the verse suggests that the words are to be taken in as terrifying a sense as possible in order that everyone should examine his own ability to erect the building.

If one thinks he can smuggle Christianity into the world by haggling, and succeeds in convincing anyone that this was the actual meaning of the passage, then he must also convince the same person that Christianity is one of the most miserable things in the world. For the most lyrical teaching, where the sense of its eternal validity swells up most strongly, offers nothing and suggests only that one is to be less kind, less attentive, more indifferent; the teaching which, just as it seems to want to tell us something terrible, ends up in drivel rather than terror — that teaching is certainly not worth standing up for.

But the words can be understood by someone who may not have the courage to do as they say. And yet there must be honesty enough to admit its greatness even if one lacks the courage oneself. In a way it contains a kind of comfort for the man who lacks courage to begin building the tower. But he must not pass off this lack of courage as humility, since it is really pride, while the courage of faith is the only humble courage.

Now, if the passage is to have any sense, it must be understood literally. God demands absolute love, but expecting someone to become lukewarm towards their loved ones as proof of their love is not only egoistic but foolish. Such a demand would ultimately lead to self-destruction, as one's own life is intertwined with the love they cherish. For instance, a husband who requires his wife to abandon her parents would be foolish to interpret her indifference towards them as a sign of her love for him. True love encompasses a wholehearted expression in all relationships, including familial ones.

But then how does one reconcile the notion of hate? Here, we won't delve into the human love/hate distinction, as it tends to be egoistic and is irrelevant in this context. Instead, if we perceive the requirement as a paradox, we can start to comprehend it as one does with paradoxes. Absolute duty might lead to actions that defy ethical norms, yet it does not imply that the knight of faith ceases to love. Abraham serves as an illustration of this paradox. When he is prepared to sacrifice Isaac, it can be said that, from an ethical standpoint, he hates his son. However, if he genuinely hated Isaac, he would realize that God does not demand such hatred, as Abraham and Cain are distinct individuals. In truth, Abraham must love Isaac with utmost intensity. When God requests Isaac's sacrifice, Abraham must love him even more, for it is this very love for Isaac that, paradoxically opposing his love for God, transforms his act into a genuine sacrifice.

Nevertheless, the distress and anguish lie in the fact that, from a human perspective, he is incapable of making himself understood. Only when his actions stand in absolute contradiction to his own emotions does he truly sacrifice Isaac. Yet the reality of his act positions him within the universal framework, where he is perceived as a murderer. The paradox lies in the tension between his individual action and the ethical norms upheld by society.

The passage in Luke must be understood in a way that recognizes the knight of faith's lack of a higher expression of the universal (the ethical) to save him. If the Church were to demand such a sacrifice from one of its members, it would result in a tragic hero. The idea of the Church is qualitatively no different from that of the State, as both require common mediation for individuals to enter. Once the individual enters the paradox, they do not attain the idea of the Church; they remain within the paradox and must find their blessedness or damnation within it. An ecclesiastical hero embodies the universal in their actions, and everyone in the Church, including their parents, understands them. However, they are not the knight of faith and do not claim it to be a trial or temptation.

People often hesitate to quote passages like the one in Luke due to a fear that unleashing individuality will lead to chaos. There is a belief that living as an individual is easy, while conforming to the universal requires coercion. I neither share this fear nor agree with this perspective, for the same reason. Those who understand that existing as an individual is the most terrifying experience will not be afraid to acknowledge its greatness. However, one must express it in a manner that guides individuals towards the universal rather than becoming a stumbling block for those who are unrestrained. While acknowledging greatness, one must also consider the needs of others. The notion that living as an individual is effortless implies a dubious admission about oneself. Those who truly respect themselves and care for their own souls understand that living in the world under one's own supervision entails greater austerity and seclusion than a maiden in her lady's chamber.

While it is true that some individuals may require coercion and would indulge in selfish pleasures without restraint, one should demonstrate through a reverent and cautious approach that they are not among them. Out of respect for greatness, one should speak about it to prevent its forgetting, despite any potential harm that may arise. Speaking as one who comprehends its greatness and terrors ensures that it is not overlooked, for without understanding its terrors, one cannot truly grasp its greatness.

Let us consider distress and fear in the paradox of faith. The tragic hero relinquishes himself to embody the universal, while the knight

of faith renounces the universal to embrace the particular. The distinction lies in their placement. Those who view individuality as an easy matter can be certain they are not knights of faith, as faith requires more than being a straggler or a wandering genius. The knight of faith understands the glory of belonging to the universal, the beauty of translating oneself into it. They strive to become a clear and elegant edition of themselves, readable and intelligible to all, finding joy in being understood and understanding the universal. Yet, they also recognize the lonely and treacherous path that lies higher up, outside the universal, where solitude prevails.

From a human perspective, the knight of faith appears insane and incomprehensible to others. "Insane" is perhaps the mildest term to describe them, and if not viewed as such, they become hypocrites. As they ascend the path, their hypocrisy becomes more dreadful. The knight of faith acknowledges the inspiration and courage found in surrendering to the universal. They understand the glory of being understood by noble minds and how such understanding ennobles the beholder. This is a task they willingly embrace, even though they feel bound by it. Abraham, for instance, must have occasionally wished that his task was to love Isaac in a conventional way, as any father would, and sacrifice him for the universal, inspiring others through his noble deed. However, he knew that such wishes were mere temptations and that his path was solitary. His actions were not for the universal but were meant to test and try him.

Abraham's journey illustrates this humanly. It took him seventy years to have the son of his old age, a joy others experience sooner. But his prolonged wait was a test. He believed, while Sarah wavered and influenced him to take Hagar as a concubine, leading to Hagar's eventual departure. When Isaac was finally born, the trials did not end. It would have been a kingly act to sacrifice his beloved son for the universal, finding solace and praise in such a deed. Yet, this was not his task; he was being tested. Comparing Abraham to the Roman general Cunctator, known for his delaying tactics, reveals the stark difference. However, Abraham was not saving a state. This span of one hundred and thirty years seems unbearable. Those around him, if they can be called contemporaries, might perceive him as an eternal procrastinator, deeming him demented. Even if he were to explain his actions, it would remain a "trial." Abraham's life is like a book seized by the divine, forever withholding public recognition.

It is a terrifying realization. Anyone who fails to see this can be certain that they are not a knight of faith. On the other hand, those who do see it cannot deny that even the most tried tragic hero's step appears like a dance compared to the slow and arduous progress of the knight of faith. Once this is acknowledged, and the courage to understand it is lacking, one can at least grasp the wonderful glory attained by the knight of faith in becoming God's confidant, the Lord's friend. In speaking humanly, it is remarkable that the knight of faith addresses God directly as "Thou," while even the tragic hero only refers to Him in the third person.

The tragic hero's journey is swiftly concluded, their struggle coming to an end as they enter the universal. In contrast, the knight of faith remains awake, constantly under trial, with the option to turn back to the universal at any moment. However, this possibility can be both a temptation and the truth, leaving the knight of faith with no external source of enlightenment on which to rely. The knight of faith, therefore, must possess an intense passion to concentrate the entirety of the ethical aspect they violate into one single thing, ensuring their genuine love for it with all their soul. If they cannot achieve this, they are in a state of temptation. Additionally, they must have the passion to evoke this certainty instantaneously and in a fully valid manner, replicating the initial experience. If they fail to do so, they must constantly restart from the beginning.

While the tragic hero can rely on the universal for assistance in acquiring these qualities, the knight of faith is alone in their endeavors. Most individuals address their ethical obligations on a daily basis but never reach the passionate concentration and energetic awareness required. The tragic hero acts and finds solace in the universal, while the knight of faith remains in constant tension. Agamemnon relinquishes his claim to Iphigenia, finding his point of rest in the universal, and proceeds to sacrifice her. If Agamemnon had not made this movement and instead became lost in casual conversations about having several daughters and the possibility of something extraordinary occurring, he would be a case for charity rather than a hero. Abraham, too, possesses the concentrated focus of a hero, although it is much more difficult for him as he lacks recourse to the universal. However, he takes one additional step to refocus his soul on the marvel. Without this action, he would merely be another Agamemnon, unless it can be justified how his willingness to sacrifice Isaac benefits the universal in a manner beyond explanation.

The distinction between a true knight of faith and a false one can be discerned even by those who are not in a state of temptation. The true knight of faith embodies absolute isolation, while the false knight adopts a sectarian mindset, attempting to cheaply emulate the role of a tragic hero. The sectarian seeks companionship and validation, surrounding themselves with like-minded individuals who represent the universal poorly. In contrast, the knight of faith embraces the paradox and remains solely an individual, free from attachments and complications. This solitary existence is unbearable for the puny sectarian. Rather than accepting their incapacity for greatness, they attempt to find solace in the company of other equally limited individuals. However, such cheating is unacceptable in the realm of the spiritual.

A dozen sectarians join forces, unaware of the lonely temptations awaiting the knight of faith, which they dare not face. The sectarians drown each other's thoughts with their cacophony, staving off their dread of the terrifying consequences of presumptuous advancement. They believe their boisterous display is akin to storming heaven, as if they are on the same path as the knight of faith, who walks in cosmic isolation, never hearing a voice, bearing his dreadful responsibility alone.

The knight of faith is assigned to himself alone, burdened with the pain of being unable to communicate effectively with others. Yet, they harbor no vain desire to guide or enlighten others. Their seriousness of mind precludes such frivolous yearnings. The false knight reveals their true nature through their immediate display of expertise. They fail to grasp that if someone else is to walk the same path, that individual must also embrace their individuality and has no need for guidance, especially from one eager to impose their services on others. Those unable to endure the martyrdom of being misunderstood abandon the path, opting instead for the world's admiration of their proficiency.

The true knight of faith is a witness, not a teacher. It is in this characteristic that their profound humanity lies, transcending the foolish preoccupation with the well-being of others masquerading as sympathy but rooted in vanity. A person who desires solely to be a witness affirms that no one, not even the most insignificant, requires another's sympathy or must be put down so another can elevate themselves. Since what the true knight has attained was not acquired easily, they do not cheapen it by accepting admiration while harboring silent contempt. They understand that true greatness is accessible to all.

Either an absolute duty to God exists, and if so, it takes the form of the paradox described—the individual as the particular surpasses the universal and shares an absolute relationship with the absolute—or faith has never truly existed because it has always existed. Otherwise, Abraham's faith becomes meaningless, or one must interpret the passage in Luke 14 as the tasteful exegete did, and similarly explain corresponding passages.

Problema III: Was it Ethically Defensible of Abraham to Conceal his Purpose from Sarah, from Eleazar, from Isaac?

The individual, in their immediate state as a sensate and psychic being, remains concealed while the ethical is universal and disclosed. Thus, their ethical task is to unveil themselves from this concealment and become manifested in the universal. Any inclination to remain concealed is a temptation and a sin, requiring disclosure for emergence.

We find ourselves at a crucial juncture once again. If there is no legitimate concealment rooted in the individual's superiority to the universal, then Abraham's actions cannot be defended, as he disregarded intermediate ethical considerations. However, if such concealment exists, we confront the unmediated paradox arising from the individual's particularity being higher than the universal, with the universal serving as the mediation. Hegelian philosophy denies justified concealment and incommensurability, remaining consistent in its demand for disclosure. Nevertheless, it is not entirely fair to consider Abraham the father of faith and discuss faith in this context. Faith is not the initial immediacy; it is a subsequent one. If faith is merely aesthetic, then it has never truly existed.

To gain a deeper understanding, let us examine the matter purely from an aesthetic perspective. We will embark on an aesthetic inquiry, and I ask the reader to wholeheartedly engage in it while I adapt my presentation accordingly. The category we will focus on is the interesting, which has acquired significant importance today, particularly in times of crisis. One should not disdain the category because it may have passed one by, nor should one be overly eager for it. To lead an interesting life, to become of interest, is a fateful privilege that can only be obtained through profound pain, as with all privileges in the realm of the spirit. Socrates, for instance, lived the most interesting life in history, but this existence was granted to him by the deity, and he endured trouble and suffering in his pursuit. Taking such an existence lightly is unbecoming for someone who takes life seriously, yet such attempts are observed nowadays.

The category of the interesting resides on the border between the aesthetic and the ethical, necessitating constant glances into the realm of ethics during our inquiry. To lend weight to our investigation, we must approach the problem with genuine aesthetic sensibility. Unfortunately, ethics often neglects such considerations these days, purportedly due to the absence of space within the System. However, exploring these topics in monographs should be acceptable, and even with brevity, the same profound insights can be achieved. A few well-chosen predicates can unveil an entire world. Are there no spaces in the System for these humble words?

According to Aristotle's Poetics, recognition (anagnorisis) in a tragedy inherently involves prior concealment. Just as recognition resolves the plot and brings relaxation to the dramatic life, concealment creates tension. In Greek tragedy, concealment and recognition stem from an epic survival rooted in a fate that obscures the origin of the dramatic action. Greek tragedy, like a sightless marble statue, requires a certain level of abstraction to be appreciated. For instance, a son unknowingly murders his father, and a sister about to sacrifice her brother realizes his true identity at the last moment. Such tragedies may be less appealing to our reflective age. Modern drama has abandoned the notion of Fate and emancipated itself in dramatic terms. It examines itself, incorporates fate into its consciousness, and explores themes of concealment and disclosure as acts of the hero's free will and responsibility.

Recognition and concealment also play crucial roles in modern drama. Although providing examples would be extensive, it is assumed that in this aesthetically indulgent age, the mere mention of concealment prompts numerous romances and comedies to come to mind. Briefly, if a character conceals something nonsensical, it results in comedy. However, if the concealment is tied to a profound idea, the concealer may approach the status of a tragic hero. Consider the comic example of a man who disguises himself with makeup and a wig to enhance his chances with women, confident in his irresistible charm. He succeeds in captivating a girl and reaches the pinnacle of joy. However, if he were to admit his deception, would he not lose his captivating allure as an ordinary, even bald-headed man? Wouldn't he have to lose the loved one once again? Concealment becomes his voluntary action, for which aesthetics holds him accountable. However, aesthetics, being unsympathetic to bald hypocrites, will subject him to the mercy of laughter. This example serves as a glimpse into the concept, recognizing that comedy cannot be fully explored within the scope of this investigation.

Concealment plays a crucial role in exploring the dialectical relationship between aesthetics and ethics. The examples provided illustrate the stark contrast between aesthetic concealment and ethical considerations. For instance, a girl secretly loves someone, but due to parental pressure, she marries another person, concealing her true feelings to avoid causing unhappiness. Similarly, a young man possesses the power to acquire his desired object with a single word, but refrains from disclosing it to prevent potential harm to an entire family. Both individuals choose concealment as a free act, for which they bear aesthetic responsibility.

Aesthetics, being a respectful and sentimental discipline, employs various means to address such situations. It orchestrates coincidences where the intended partners in arranged marriages discover the noble decisions of the concealed lovers. Explanations ensue, resulting in the union of the true lovers and their elevation to the status of heroes. Although they have not had the opportunity to reflect on their resolutions, aesthetics perceives their actions as if they had valiantly fought for their love over many years. Time holds little significance for aesthetics, whether in jest or earnest.

On the other hand, ethics remains oblivious to coincidences or sentimentalities. It operates based on pure categories, impervious to experiential factors that can be laughable and even drive a person to madness if they lack a higher understanding. Ethics does not provide explanations or flirt with notions of dignity. Instead, it burdens the fragile shoulders of the hero with immense responsibility. It condemns the hero's presumption to play the role of providence in their actions and likewise condemns them for attempting to do the same with their suffering. Ethics emphasizes belief in reality and encourages courage in facing its tribulations, rather than focusing on the self-imposed sufferings borne out of personal responsibility. It warns against misplaced magnanimity and cautions against placing undue trust in the cunning of reason, which is more treacherous than ancient oracles. Courage should be displayed when reality dictates the occasion. In such instances, ethics stands ready to offer assistance.

However, if there had been a deeper sense of purpose and a genuine commitment to the task at hand within the concealed individuals, something meaningful may have emerged. Yet, ethics is incapable of aiding them. It is offended because they keep a secret from it, a secret for which they alone bear responsibility.

Thus, aesthetics advocates for concealment and rewards it, while ethics calls for disclosure and punishes concealment.

Sometimes, even aesthetics calls for disclosure. When a hero, trapped in an aesthetic illusion, believes that their silence can save another, aesthetics rewards and advocates for silence. However, when the hero's actions involve interfering in someone else's life, disclosure becomes necessary. This is particularly true in the case of tragic heroes, exemplified by Agamemnon in Euripides's Iphigenia in Aulis. Aesthetics calls for Agamemnon's silence, as it would be unworthy for the hero to seek consolation from others, and it is better to keep the truth hidden for the sake of the women involved. Nevertheless, the hero must also face the terrible temptation posed by the tears of Clytemnestra and Iphigenia to be tested as a true hero. Aesthetics resolves this contradiction by introducing an old servant who discloses everything to Clytemnestra, thereby fulfilling the aesthetic ideal.

Ethics, however, does not rely on coincidences or convenient servants. The application of the aesthetic idea in reality reveals its self-contradictory nature. Ethics demands disclosure in such situations. The tragic hero displays ethical courage by refusing to be captive to the aesthetic illusion and taking it upon themselves to reveal Iphigenia's fate. In this act, the tragic hero becomes the beloved son of ethics, pleasing her. The hero's silence may be intended to ease the burden for others or even for themselves, but they know they are free from selfish motives. By remaining silent, they assume individual responsibility, as they are impervious to external arguments. However, as a tragic hero, they cannot do so because it is by expressing the universal that ethics embraces them. Their heroic action requires courage, and part of that courage lies in not shying away from any argument. Tears, indeed, can be a powerful argumentum ad hominem, capable of stirring even the most resistant individuals. The play allows Iphigenia to weep, suggesting that, like Jephthah's daughter, she should have been granted time to weep at her father's feet.

Aesthetics demanded disclosure but relied on a fortunate coincidence, while ethics required disclosure and found satisfaction in the tragic hero's actions. Despite the stringent ethical demand for disclosure, it cannot be denied that secrecy and silence, as manifestations of inner emotions, contribute to greatness in a person. In the story of Amor and Psyche, Amor tells her that her child will be divine if she keeps the secret, but human if she betrays it. The tragic hero, the favorite of ethics, is purely human, someone whose intentions are transparent. Going further, one encounters the paradox of silence, embodying both the demonic and the divine. Silence entices like a demon, and the more one remains silent, the more terrifying the demon becomes. However, silence is also the means through which one individually communes with divinity.

Before returning to the story of Abraham, there is a desire to introduce some poetic characters. By subjecting them to dialectical analysis, keeping them at extremes, and invoking despair, they might unveil something in their anguish.

Aristotle recounts a political disturbance in Delphi caused by a canceled wedding. The groom, warned by the augurs of an impending misfortune, changes his mind and refuses to proceed with the marriage at the last moment. This event, though brief, surely evoked tears in Delphi and could be the subject of a poet's sympathetic portrayal. It is a tragic irony that love, often considered heavenly, is here deprived of celestial intervention. The notion that marriages are ordained in heaven is challenged in this case. Typically, the trials of human existence seek to separate lovers, while love itself is supported by the heavens, triumphing over all adversaries. Yet, in this instance, heaven itself severs the union it had supposedly blessed. No one, especially not the young bride, could have anticipated this outcome. Moments earlier, she had been in her room, radiating beauty, as her companions adorned her with utmost care. Their craftsmanship surpassed mere happiness and incited envy, albeit a joyful envy that couldn't be surpassed, given her unparalleled beauty. Alone in her room, she underwent a transformation, as all her feminine artistry adorned her virtuous character. However, there was still something missing—something the young girl had not envisioned. It was a veil, ethereal and elusive, surpassing the one bestowed upon her by her maids. None of them possessed knowledge of this veil or could assist her with it; even the bride herself was unaware of how to don it. This unseen and benevolent force delighted in adorning the bride, enwrapping her without her awareness. All she saw was the bridegroom passing by on his way to the temple. She witnessed him enter, and her tranquility and bliss deepened, knowing that he now belonged to her more than ever. The temple door opened, and he emerged, his troubled countenance hidden from her demure gaze. Yet, he perceived that heaven envied the bride's beauty and his own good fortune. The temple door opened again, and the young maids saw the bridegroom's exit, oblivious to the turmoil on his face as they busied themselves with escorting the bride. She, displaying maidenly modesty, stood at the forefront, akin to a mistress attended by her retinue of young maids of honor, who respectfully curtsied before her. Standing poised with her lovely entourage, she awaited the groom's arrival, knowing the temple was nearby. However, he passed by her door.

Here, I digress. I am not a poet, but a practitioner of dialectics. We must first note that the hero learns of the impending misfortune at a critical moment, allowing him to remain blameless and unbound to the loved one. Secondly, the utterance he faces is divine, or rather, against him, freeing him from conceited behavior displayed by weak lovers. Naturally, this utterance brings him unhappiness, surpassing even that of the bride, as he is the cause of it all. Although the augurs only predicted misfortune for him, it raises the question of whether this misfortune may also affect their marital bliss. So, what are his options? (1) Should he remain silent, proceed with the wedding, and think, 'Perhaps the misfortune won't occur immediately, and in any case, I have remained faithful to my love, unafraid to embrace unhappiness. But I must remain silent, preserving even this fleeting moment.' While this may sound plausible, it is far from ideal, as it would insult the girl. By keeping silent, he indirectly implicates her, as she would never have consented to such a union if she knew the truth. In his hour of need, he would not only bear the misfortune but also the responsibility for his silence, facing her rightful anger for withholding the truth. (2) Should he remain silent and not marry? In that case, he must engage in a deception that erases himself from their relationship. Aesthetics might appreciate this approach, allowing the catastrophe to unfold similarly to the real story, with explanations offered at the last moment, although it would be too late, aesthetically necessitating his demise—unless the discipline of aesthetics could intervene and nullify the fateful prophecy. However noble this conduct may seem, it insults the girl and the authenticity of her love. (3) Should he speak? Naturally, we must remember that our hero is a bit too poetic for the abandonment of his love to have no significance beyond a failed venture. If he speaks, the entire affair transforms into an unfortunate love story akin to Axel and Valborg. They become a couple separated by heaven itself. Nevertheless, in this case, their separation is conceived differently, as it also stems from the free actions of the individuals. The challenge lies in the fact that the misfortune is to affect only him. Unlike Axel and Valborg, who find a shared expression of their suffering, as heaven equally separates them due to their closeness, a resolution becomes elusive. If that were the case here, a way out could be envisioned. Since heaven employs no visible power to separate them, but leaves the choice to the individuals, one could imagine their defiance of heaven, uniting despite its misfortune.

Ethics demand that our hero speaks. The essence of his bravery lies in relinquishing his lofty aesthetic ideals, devoid of any vain concealment, knowing that he still causes the girl unhappiness. The reality of this heroism hinges on the cancellation of its presupposition - that he genuinely loved her and remained silent for her sake, not his. Otherwise, we would encounter countless heroes, especially in our time, which excels in forgery that skips over the essential in-between.

However, why this exposition if it merely culminates in the tragic hero? Because it may shed light on the paradox. It all depends on our hero's relationship to the augur's utterance, which will inevitably shape his life's course. Is this utterance public property or a private matter? Set in Greece, an augur's words are intelligible to all—not just lexically, but in the sense that individuals understand it as a decision from heaven. The augur's utterance is comprehensible not only to the hero but to everyone, establishing no private connection to the divine. Wherever he turns, the prophecy will come true, irrespective of his actions or inactions. He won't attain a closer relationship with the divine, nor become an object of divine mercy or wrath, regardless of his choices. The outcome will be as understandable to anyone as it is to the hero, with no secret code reserved solely for him. Thus, should he desire to speak, he can do so effectively, making himself understood. And if he opts for silence, it is because he wishes, as an individual, to surpass the universal, deluding himself with fantasies of her eventual recovery from sorrow, and so on.

On the other hand, if the will of heaven had been communicated to him in a private manner, establishing an intimate relationship, then we encounter the paradox - assuming it exists (since my reflections here adopt a dilemma format) - in this scenario, he would be unable to speak, no matter how much he desires to. He would not find solace in his silence, but endure the pain, yet for him, this would be the confirmation that he acted rightly. Therefore, the reason for his silence would not be to establish himself as the singular individual in an absolute relation to the universal, but to be placed as the singular individual in an absolute relationship with the absolute. To my understanding, he would also find tranquility in this, whereas the demands of the ethical would perpetually disturb his lofty silence. It is hoped that aesthetics could initiate where it has long concluded - with the illusion of high-mindedness. By doing so, it would collaborate with religion, as the sole force capable of resolving the aesthetic's conflict with the ethical.

Queen Elizabeth sacrificed her love for Essex to the State by signing his death warrant. That act was heroic, even if some personal resentment played a role because he hadn't sent her the ring. We know that he did send it, but it was maliciously withheld by a lady-in-waiting. Elizabeth is said, if I am not mistaken, to have been informed of this and spent ten days biting one finger in silence before her eventual demise. This anecdote would captivate a poet skilled in prying open closed mouths, though it may, at best, serve a ballet master, as the poet nowadays often confuses himself with the latter.

I want to present a sketch that delves into the demonic, using the legend of Agnete and the Merman. Traditionally, the merman is portrayed as a seducer who emerges from the depths to break the innocent flower by the shore. Let's alter the narrative. The merman, a seducer, entices Agnete, extracting her innermost thoughts with his smooth words. Agnete finds in him what she sought, peering into the sea's depths. Willingly, she follows him down, wrapping her arms around his neck and surrendering her soul to the stronger entity. At the water's edge, as he prepares to dive with his prey, Agnete gazes at him not with fear, pride, or intoxicated desire, but with unwavering faith and absolute humility, like the humble flower she perceives herself to be. With complete trust, she entrusts her entire fate to him.

Surprisingly, the ocean falls silent, nature's passion - the merman's strength - abandons him, and the sea becomes calm. Agnete continues to look at him this way. Overwhelmed by the power of innocence, the merman collapses; his element betrays him, and he cannot seduce Agnete. He guides her back home, explaining that he merely wanted to show her the serene beauty of the sea, and Agnete believes him. Alone, he returns to the raging ocean, consumed by even greater despair. He can seduce countless Agnetes, enchant any girl, but Agnete has triumphed, and the merman has lost her. She can only become his prize, for he cannot faithfully belong to any girl, being merely a merman.

I have slightly modified both the merman and Agnete. In the legend, Agnete is not innocent - she yearns for the intriguing and attracts the attention of mermen who prey upon such desires. It is foolish to assume that refinement protects a girl from seduction; innocence alone offers true protection. Now, we assign human consciousness to the merman, suggesting a previous human existence that entangles his life. Despite his past, he can become a hero through a reconciliatory act. Saved by Agnete, he is crushed as the seducer, yielding to the power of innocence and forever losing his ability to seduce. Yet, two forces vie for control over him: repentance alone or repentance with Agnete. If repentance alone prevails, he remains hidden, but if repentance and Agnete take hold, he is revealed.

As the sea roars and waves foam, the merman embraces Agnete and dives into the depths. He has never been so wild or consumed by desire, as he hoped she would be his deliverance. However, he soon grows weary of Agnete, and her body is never found. She transforms into a mermaid, luring men with her songs.

If the merman succumbs to repentance alone and remains hidden, he will undoubtedly make Agnete unhappy. In her innocence, Agnete loved him and believed in his momentary change, even if he concealed it well, when he claimed he only wanted to show her the tranquil beauty of the sea. On the other hand, the merman himself becomes even more miserable when it comes to passion. He loved Agnete intensely, and now he bears the burden of guilt. The demonic aspect of repentance will likely tell him that this is his punishment, and the more it torments him, the more justified it feels.

If he gives in to this demonic possibility, he may attempt to save Agnete in a twisted way, using evil means. Knowing that Agnete loves him, he believes that by tearing away her love, he can somehow save her. But how can he achieve that? The merman is too sensible to believe that a candid confession would repulse her. Instead, he might try to awaken dark passions within her, scorn her, mock her, and ridicule her love, even attempting to stir up her pride. He will spare himself no torment, as this is the deep contradiction inherent in the demonic. Paradoxically, there is infinitely more good in the demonic than in a superficial person. The more self-centered Agnete is, the easier it will be to deceive her (only those with little experience believe it is easy to deceive innocence; life is profound, and it is the astute who excel in deceiving one another). However, the merman will suffer all the more intensely. The more ingeniously he contrives his deception, the less Agnete will shy away from revealing her own pain to him. She will use every means at her disposal, not to push him away, but to torment him.

Through the demonic, the merman aspires to be the singular individual who, in particularity, rises above the universal. Like the divine, the demonic allows the individual to enter into an absolute relationship with it. This bears some resemblance to the paradox we are discussing, which can be misleading. The merman appears to have proof that his silence is justified because it is the source of his suffering. However, there is no doubt that he can speak. If he does, he can become a tragic hero, a truly grand tragic hero in my opinion. Perhaps only a few will understand the magnitude of his greatness. He will then have the courage to free himself from the self-deception that he can make Agnete happy through his art. He will have the courage, in human terms, to crush Agnete. Here, I will add a psychological observation. The more self-centered we make Agnete, the more effective the self-deception will be. It is not inconceivable that, with his demonic astuteness, the merman might have, in reality, not only saved Agnete but brought out something exceptional in her. A demon knows how to extract powers even from the weakest person, and in his own way, he can have the best intentions towards a human being.

The merman finds himself at a dialectical extreme. If he is saved from the demonic side of repentance, two paths lie before him. He can hold himself back, remain concealed, but without relying on his astuteness. In this case, he does not enter into an absolute relationship with the demonic as the singular individual, but instead finds solace in the counter-paradox that the divine will save Agnete. This aligns with the medieval notion, as the merman has seemingly dedicated himself to the monastery. Alternatively, he can be saved through Agnete. However, this does not mean that Agnete's love will save him from being a seducer in the future, as that would be an aesthetic attempt to rescue him, avoiding the main issue of the merman's life's continuity. In that aspect, he is already saved. He will be saved through disclosure. Thus, he marries Agnete. Yet, he still must rely on the paradox. When the individual has emerged from the universal due to their own guilt, they can only return to it by entering into an absolute relationship with the absolute as the particular. At this point, I will introduce a comment that takes us beyond anything discussed previously. Sin is not the initial immediacy; sin is a subsequent immediacy. In sin, the individual is already, in terms of the demonic paradox, higher than the universal because it is a contradiction for the universal to impose itself on someone lacking the necessary condition. If philosophy, among its many conceits, imagines that someone might genuinely follow its precepts in practice, a curious comedy would ensue. An ethics that disregards sin is ultimately a futile discipline, but once it postulates sin, it has inherently transcended itself. Philosophy teaches us to transcend the immediate, and while that is true, it is also true that sin, like faith, is not simply the immediate.

Everything progresses smoothly within these realms, but even with all that has been said, it still does not fully explain Abraham. Abraham did not become the singular individual through sin; on the contrary, he was the righteous man chosen by God. Therefore, any analogy with Abraham will only surface once the individual becomes capable of accomplishing the universal, and now the paradox is repeated.

The movements of the merman can be understood, but understanding Abraham is a different matter. The merman turns to the paradox in order to realize the universal. If he remains hidden and dedicates himself to the torments of repentance, he becomes a demon and is ultimately destroyed. If he stays hidden without entertaining the idea of saving Agnete at the cost of his own torment, he may find peace but is lost to the world. If he reveals himself and allows himself to be saved through Agnete, then he becomes the greatest human being imaginable. Only aesthetics mistakenly believes that the power of love can be praised by allowing the lost man to be loved and saved by an innocent girl. It confuses the roles and fails to recognize that the merman is the true hero. Therefore, the merman cannot belong to Agnete until he has gone through the infinite movement of repentance and then made one more movement based on the absurd. His own strength is sufficient for the movement of repentance, but it requires all of his energy. Thus, it is impossible for him to return to reality by his own strength alone. If one lacks the passion to make either movement and merely goes through life, repenting a little and expecting everything to work out, they have given up on living in the idea and it becomes easy to reach the highest level of delusion, where one believes that everyone cheats in the world of spirit, akin to a card game. It is interesting to reflect on how, in an age when everyone can supposedly reach the highest, there is widespread doubt about the immortality of the soul. Those who have genuinely made the movement of infinity can hardly be called doubters. The conclusions of passion are the only reliable and convincing ones. Fortunately, life is kinder and more faithful than the wise would have it. It does not exclude anyone, not even the humblest, and it does not deceive anyone. In the world of spirit, the only ones who are deceived are those who deceive themselves. Entering the monastery is not considered the highest pursuit, but that does not mean that the souls who found repose there in the past were any less profound or earnest. How many individuals in our age have the passion to genuinely contemplate such thoughts and judge themselves honestly? The idea of taking time for introspection, allowing conscience to search out every secret thought with unwavering perseverance, and facing the dark passions concealed within oneself can be chastening. This idea alone should be enough to humble many individuals in an age that believes it has already reached the highest.

This age, which believes it has reached the pinnacle, pays little attention to these concerns, even though no era has fallen so victim to the comic as ours. It's perplexing why this age hasn't yet spontaneously given birth to its own hero, a demon who fearlessly stages a horrifying play that reduces the entire era to laughter, oblivious to the fact that it is laughing at itself. What value does life hold when people believe they have already achieved everything by the age of twenty? And what significant progress has this age made since people stopped entering monasteries? It is a contemptible worldliness, a cautious and cowardly approach that sits at the head of the table, cunningly convincing people they have reached the highest and dissuading them from striving for anything less. Those who have embarked on the path of the monastery have only one movement left—the movement of the absurd. How many nowadays truly comprehend the absurd? How many live in a way that they have renounced or gained everything? How many are simply honest enough to recognize their own limitations and capabilities? And if there are such individuals, they are mostly found among the less educated and, to some extent, among women. Just as a demonic person unwittingly reveals themselves, our age exposes its own deficiencies through a kind of clairvoyance, always yearning for the comic. If that is truly what it needs, perhaps the theater should present a new play treating someone's death for love as comedy. Or would it be better for our age to actually witness such an event, so it may gather the courage to believe in the power of the spirit and cease suppressing its better impulses, and to stop stifling them in others with laughter? Does this age truly require a ridiculous spectacle of an enthusiast to mock? Or does it, in reality, need such an enthusiastic figure to remind it of what it has forgotten?

For a similar scenario but with a more poignant touch, one can turn to the story of Tobias in the Book of Tobit. Tobias desires to marry

Sarah, who has experienced great tragedy. She had been betrothed to seven men, all of whom died on their wedding nights. Although this aspect of the story has a comical quality, it detracts from the tragic effect I seek to portray. Therefore, in my version, Sarah is a girl who has never been in love, holding onto a young girl's ideal of happiness, her unwavering hope to love a man wholeheartedly. Yet, she is the most wretched of all, burdened by the knowledge that the demon who loves her will kill her bridegrooms. I have encountered much sorrow, but I doubt there exists a sorrow as profound as hers. When misfortune befalls someone from external circumstances, there is a certain solace. Even if life fails to grant a person what would bring them happiness, it is still comforting to know it could have been possible. But the immeasurable sorrow that time cannot dispel or heal is the realization that even if life were to grant everything, it would be in vain! A Greek author captures the essence with crude naiveté, saying, "...for certainly no one has yet altogether escaped love, and none shall so long as there is beauty and eyes to see" (cf. Longus' Daphnis and Chloe). Many girls have experienced unhappiness in love, but they became unhappy; Sarah was unhappy before it even began. It is difficult enough not to find someone to whom one can devote oneself, but it is incomprehensibly difficult to be unable to devote oneself. A young girl surrenders herself to someone, and then it is said she is no longer free, but Sarah was never free and yet never surrendered herself to anyone. It is difficult enough for a girl to surrender herself to someone and be deceived by love, but Sarah was deceived even before she surrendered. The depth of sorrow becomes evident when Tobias finally decides to marry Sarah. The wedding rituals and preparations unfold, and no girl has ever been as deceived as Sarah. She is robbed of the most precious of all treasures: the absolute wealth that even the poorest girl possesses—the secure, boundless, unreserved surrender of devotion. The purification ritual involves placing the heart and liver of a fish on glowing embers. And what a heart-wrenching farewell between mother and daughter, where both have been deprived of everything—the daughter must also deprive her mother of her most beautiful possession. We read the account: Edna prepares the chamber, brings Sarah inside, weeps, and receives her daughter's tears. She consoles her, saying, "My child, take heart. The Lord of heaven and earth may exchange your sorrow for joy. Daughter, take heart." And now, the moment of the wedding. We continue reading, if we can through our tears: "But when the door was shut and they were together, Tobias rose from the bed and said, 'Rise up, sister, and we will pray that the Lord may have mercy on us'" (8.4).

If a poet were to read this story and use it, I am certain they would focus on the young Tobias as the hero. His bravery in risking his life, as emphasized in the narrative when Raguel tells Edna the morning after the wedding to send a maid to check if Tobias is still alive, would be the poet's theme. However, I propose a different perspective. While Tobias acted with gallantry and determination, any man lacking the courage to do so is a coward who knows neither the essence of love nor the essence of being a man. Such a man fails to grasp the small mystery that giving is better than receiving and remains oblivious to the greater mystery that receiving is much harder than giving, particularly if one has the courage to go without and not be a coward in times of need. No, the true heroine is Sarah. I feel drawn to her in a way I have never been drawn to any other girl or even contemplated in thought about any girl I have read about. The love for God it takes to desire healing when one has been crippled from birth, an unsuccessful specimen of humanity through no fault of one's own, is remarkable. The ethical maturity to accept the responsibility of allowing the loved one to undertake such a daring act, the humility before another person, and the faith in God that prevents her from hating the man to whom she owes everything—these qualities make Sarah the true heroine.

When Sarah becomes a man, the demonic is not far away. A proud and noble nature can endure anything except pity. Pity implies an indignity that can only be inflicted from above upon such an individual, for he himself can never become an object of pity. If he has sinned, he can bear the punishment without despair, but being singled out from birth as an object of pity, a sweet fragrance to pity's nostrils, he cannot endure. Pity has a peculiar dialectic: at one moment, it demands guilt, and the next, it seeks to abolish it. Thus, to be destined for pity is more dreadful when the individual's misfortune lies in the spiritual realm. But Sarah bears no guilt; she is subjected to every form of suffering and, on top of that, tortured by human sympathy. Even I, who admire her more than Tobias loves her, cannot mention her name without exclaiming, "The poor girl!" If a man were to take Sarah's place, knowing that loving a girl would invite a demonic spirit to murder her on the wedding night, he would likely choose the demonic path, withdraw into himself, and, like the demonic nature, say in his heart, "Thanks, I have no interest in ceremony and fuss. I don't need the pleasures of love; I can just as well be a Bluebeard who finds pleasure in witnessing the death of girls on their wedding night."

The demonic is a subject rarely discussed, despite its relevance in our time. Once one understands how to establish a certain rapport with the demon, an observer can use almost anyone as an example in some respect. In this regard, Shakespeare remains a heroic figure. The most demonic character Shakespeare ever portrayed, Gloucester (later Richard III), became a demon because he could not bear the pity that had been heaped upon him since childhood. His monologue in the first act of King Richard III holds more value than all moral systems, as none of them hint at the existential terrors and their nature.

I, that am rudely stamped, and want love's majesty

To strut before a wanton ambling nymph;

I, that am curtailed of this fair proportion,

Cheated of feature by dissembling nature,

Deformed, unfinished, sent before my time

Into this breathing world scarce half made up,

And that so lamely and unfashionable

That dogs bark at me as I halt by them ...

Nature's like Gloucester's cannot be saved by mediating them into an idea of society. Ethics mocks them, just as it would mock Sarah if it suggested she express the universal and get married. Such natures are inherently paradoxical and no less perfect than others; they are either damned in the demonic paradox or delivered in the divine. Throughout history, people have mistakenly associated misshapen creatures like witches, gnomes, and trolls with moral perversion. But this is a colossal injustice. Life itself corrupts them, much like a stepmother corrupts her stepchildren. Being excluded from the universal from the beginning, either by nature or historical circumstances, is the starting point of the demonic, and the individual cannot be blamed for that. Even Cumberland's Jew is a demon despite his beneficence. The demonic can manifest as contempt for humanity, although it is important to note that the demonic person himself does not act contemptuously. On the contrary, their strength lies in knowing they are superior to those who judge them.

Poets should be the first to stir up discussions on these matters. Who knows what books our young poets are reading nowadays? Perhaps they only learn to recite rhymes by heart. Their significance in life is a mystery to me. Right now, I cannot honestly tell you if they are good for anything other than providing proof of the immortality of the soul, to the extent that one can safely say of them what Baggesen said of the city's poet, Kildevalle: "If he is immortal, then we all are." The poetic portrayal of Sarah presented here, appealing to the imagination, gains full significance when we explore the meaning of the old saying: "nullum unquam exstitit magnum ingenium sine aliqua dementia" (there was never great genius without some madness). The dementia mentioned here is the genius's suffering in life, the expression of divine jealousy, while genius itself is the mark of divine favor. Thus, the genius is disoriented from the beginning in relation to the universal and placed in relation to the paradox. In despair over their own limitations, which turn their omnipotence into impotence, they may seek demonic reassurance and refuse to acknowledge limitations before God or man. Alternatively, they may find religious reassurance through love for the divine. The psychological topics touched upon here are worthy of a lifetime of exploration, yet they are rarely discussed. How is madness connected to genius? Can one be constructed from the other? In what way and to what extent does the genius have control over their own madness? It is evident that they possess some degree of control, or else they would truly be mad. However, making such observations requires a high level of ingenuity and love, as it is exceedingly difficult to observe individuals of superior talent. When reading the works of celebrated authors known for their genius, one must keep this in mind and exert great effort to uncover something meaningful occasionally.

I will now explore another case of an individual seeking to save the universal through concealment and silence, focusing on the legend of Faust. Typically, Faust is portrayed as a doubter, a spiritual apostate who indulges in worldly desires. This interpretation has been reiterated by poets throughout the ages, despite the claim that every era has its own Faust. However, let us slightly alter our perspective. Faust is indeed a doubter, but he possesses a sympathetic nature. Even Goethe's portrayal of Faust lacks a deeper psychological understanding of the internal conversations doubt engages in with itself. In the present day, when doubt is a universal experience, no poet has ventured into exploring this aspect. I am tempted to offer poets Royal Securities to write down all they have experienced regarding doubt, as it is unlikely that their accounts would occupy more than the left-hand margin of the page.

Only when we turn Faust's introspective gaze upon himself can doubt manifest poetically, and only then does he genuinely discover the sufferings it entails. He recognizes that spirit sustains life, but also understands that the security and happiness people enjoy are not upheld by the power of spirit; rather, they can be attributed to unreflective bliss. As a doubter, Faust stands above such things. If someone tries to deceive him into thinking he has overcome doubt, he easily discerns the truth. Like an individual who has traversed the world of spirit and undergone an infinite journey, Faust can instantly distinguish between an experienced speaker and a Münchhausen-like fabricator. Faust realizes that just as Tamerlane could command fear in his adversaries, he too can instill terror in people, making the world tremble beneath their feet, causing them to scatter in panic and triggering alarm in every corner. And yet, Faust is not a mere conqueror; possessing the authority of thought, he is justified in such actions. However, Faust possesses a sympathetic nature, he cherishes life, harbors no envy, and recognizes his inability to prevent the impending catastrophe that doubt may unleash. He does not seek Herostratic honor; instead, he remains silent, diligently concealing his doubt within his soul, much like a girl concealing the fruit of her illicit love within her womb. Faust attempts to synchronize with others as best he can outwardly, but internally he consumes the turmoil, sacrificing himself to the universal.

Sometimes, when an eccentric individual stirs up a whirlwind of doubt, one might hear the complaint, "If only they had remained quiet." Faust embodies this sentiment. Those who understand the profound implications of living through spirit also comprehend the hunger for doubt, as doubters yearn not only for spiritual nourishment but also for the daily bread of life. While the pain Faust endures serves as evidence against his being driven by pride, I will employ a precautionary device. It is within my grasp, considering that I, who might be tempted to call myself "tortor heroum" (the torturer of heroes) similar to how Gregory of Rimini was labeled "tortor infantium" due to his belief in the damnation of infants, am quite inventive in tormenting heroes. Faust encounters Marguerite not after he chooses a life of pleasure—my Faust does not choose pleasure at all—but rather, he sees Marguerite in all her lovable innocence, not through Mephistopheles's distorted mirror. And because his soul still holds love for humanity, he can genuinely fall in love with her. However, he is a doubter, and doubt has eroded reality for him. My Faust is an idealist, not merely a scientific doubter who questions during lectures but remains unaffected in everyday life. He hungers for both the sustenance of spirit and the daily joys of life. Yet, he remains faithful to his decision, maintaining his silence and refraining from discussing his doubt or confessing his love to Marguerite.

It is evident that Faust is too ideal a figure to be satisfied with the notion that speaking up would only trigger a general discussion, or that the matter would blow over without consequences. Here lies the dormant comedy in our scenario, which, as any poet can see, places Faust in an ironic relationship with those fools who chase doubt, offering external proofs such as doctor's certificates to demonstrate their doubt or swearing oaths that they have doubted everything, or even proving their doubt by claiming to have encountered a fellow doubter on their journey. These individuals act as express couriers and sprint experts in the realm of spirit, hastily collecting fragments of doubt from one person and snippets of faith from another, engaging in business transactions according to the demands of their audience, whether they prefer fine or coarse sand. Faust is too ideal to walk about in slippers. An ideal figure lacks an infinite passion, and those who possess an infinite passion have long liberated their souls from such trivialities. Faust remains silent, either to offer himself up or to disrupt everything with his words.

He remains silent, and ethics condemns him for it. Ethics dictates that one must acknowledge the universal by speaking, without showing pity for it. This should be kept in mind when harshly judging a doubter who chooses to speak. Personally, I am not inclined to be lenient in such cases, but the key lies in proper movements. Even if by speaking, a doubter brings misfortune upon the world, they would still be preferable to those miserable individuals who indulge in everything, attempting to cure doubt without truly understanding it. Such individuals often become the catalysts for outbreaks of uncontrollable doubt. Speaking confuses everything, as the doubter only realizes that nothing has changed afterward, and this realization offers no assistance in the moment or in matters of responsibility.

By choosing silence, the doubter may act magnanimously, but they face the additional temptation of the universal constantly plaguing them, questioning whether their decision was driven by hidden pride. If the doubter can be the singular individual who, in their particularity, establishes an absolute relation to the absolute, they receive authorization for their silence. However, they must then make guilt of their doubt. They enter the realm of paradox, where doubt may be cured, yet they can acquire new doubts.

Even the New Testament would approve of such silence. There are passages in the New Testament that extol irony, as long as it serves to conceal the better side. This movement of irony is just as valid as any other movement based on subjectivity surpassing reality. Unfortunately, contemporary society does not desire to explore irony beyond what Hegel has already discussed, despite his limited understanding and resentment toward it. The age guards itself against irony, viewing it as a threat. The Sermon on the Mount advises: "But thou, when thou fastest, anoint thine head, and wash thy face; that thou appear not unto men to fast." This passage testifies to the incomprehensibility of subjectivity in relation to reality, even granting it the right to deceive. If only those who currently wander about discussing vague notions of the congregation would read the New Testament, they might encounter different ideas.

Now, let us consider Abraham. How did he act? It is essential to remember that the entire preceding discussion has led to this point. Not to make Abraham more understandable, but to highlight his incomprehensibility. I confess, I cannot understand Abraham; I can only admire him. None of the stages described previously resemble Abraham; they were presented only to illustrate, within their respective realms, the boundaries of the unknown land through their points of discrepancy. If there were any analogy, it would have to be the paradox of sin. However, that belongs to a different sphere and cannot explain Abraham. Moreover, it is much easier to explain the paradox of sin than to comprehend Abraham.

Abraham's silence was notable, as he refrained from speaking to Sarah, Eleazar, and Isaac. He bypassed these ethical authorities because, for him, the ethical realm found no higher expression than family life. Aesthetics demanded silence from individuals when it could save another, but Abraham's silence was not to save Isaac. Sacrificing Isaac for his own and God's sake was aesthetically outrageous. The aesthetic hero chose silence, but ethics condemned him for remaining silent based on his accidental particularity. Human prescience played a role in his silence, but ethics cannot forgive such insight as it demands disclosure through infinite movement. The tragic hero sacrifices everything for the universal and is beloved by ethics, but this does not apply to Abraham. He does not act for the universal and remains concealed.

Now we face the paradox. Either the individual as the particular can have an absolute relation to the absolute, making the ethical not the highest, or Abraham is left without being a tragic or aesthetic hero. However, one should not view the paradox as easy or convenient. Distress and anguish are the only justifications, even if they cannot be fully comprehended, for if they could, the paradox would be eliminated.

Abraham is silent, but he cannot speak. Here lies the distress and anguish. Even if he keeps talking incessantly, if he cannot make himself understood, he does not truly speak. Abraham can express his love for Isaac in beautiful language, but that is not his deeper thought of sacrificing Isaac as a trial. No one can understand this, leading to misunderstanding the former statement. The tragic hero is unaware of this distress. They find solace in addressing all counter-arguments, providing an opportunity for every voice and thought to challenge them. Engaging with the whole world is comforting, but contending with oneself is dreadful. The tragic hero need not fear overlooking anything, unlike King Edward IV upon learning of Clarence's death.

Who pleaded for him? Who, in my anger, knelt and advised caution? Who spoke of brotherhood? Who spoke of love?

The tragic hero remains oblivious to the weight of solitary responsibility. Furthermore, they find solace in weeping and lamenting with Clytemnestra and Iphigenia. Crying brings relief, while unutterable groans inflict torment. Agamemnon quickly gathers himself, certain of his actions, and has time to offer comfort and courage. Abraham lacks this ability. When his heart stirs and his words could bring solace to the world, he dares not console. Sarah, Eleazar, and Isaac would question his intentions, suggesting he could refrain. If he were to unburden himself and embrace his loved ones before taking the final step, it could lead to Sarah, Eleazar, and Isaac finding offense and believing him a hypocrite. He cannot speak, for he communicates in a divine tongue, beyond human language, even if he understood all tongues of the world.

His distress is understandable, and Abraham is admirable. Yet, I confess my own lack of courage for such a path. I would willingly renounce further progress if only I could reach that level, however late it may be. Abraham has the option to refrain and repent at any moment, viewing it as a temptation. Then he can speak, and all will understand him, but he would cease to be Abraham.

Abraham cannot articulate the explanation for everything, that it is a trial—a trial in which the ethical becomes the temptation. He cannot express it in a way that can be understood. In such a predicament, one becomes estranged from the realm of the universal. Furthermore, he is even less capable of articulating what comes next. As established earlier, Abraham makes two movements. He makes the infinite movement of resignation, relinquishing his claim to Isaac, which is incomprehensible because it is a personal endeavor. However, he also continually makes the movement of faith. This is his solace. He asserts, "Nevertheless, it won't happen, or if it does, the Lord will provide a new Isaac based on the absurd." The tragic hero at least reaches the end of the story. Iphigenia accepts her father's decision and herself makes the infinite movement of resignation, enabling mutual understanding. She comprehends Agamemnon because his action expresses the universal. If, on the other hand, Agamemnon were to say, "Even though the deity demands your sacrifice, it's still possible that he didn't, based on the absurd," he would instantly become unintelligible to her. If he could express it through human calculation, Iphigenia would surely understand. However, that would mean Agamemnon had not made the infinite movement of resignation, rendering him no hero. In that case, the seer's prophecy becomes mere folklore, and the entire incident becomes a farce.

Abraham remained silent, except for one preserved word—his only reply to Isaac. This single word holds great significance and plays a crucial role in the entire incident. I often pondered whether a tragic hero, in the culmination of their heroism through suffering or action, should have a final remark. The answer lies in the sphere of life they belong to, the intellectual significance of their existence, and the relationship between their suffering or action and the realm of spirit.

If the hero's life revolves around an outward act, then there is no need for them to speak, as their words would be mere idle chatter, diminishing the impact they have made. Tragic rites demand that they fulfill their task in silence, whether through action or suffering. Consider Agamemnon: had he been the one to wield the knife on Iphigenia instead of Calchas, uttering a few words in the final moment would have demeaned his act. The significance of his deed was already understood, and his life had no connection to the realm of spirit; he was neither a teacher nor a witness to the spirit.

However, if the hero's life bears relevance to spirit, the absence of a final remark weakens their impact. It is not a matter of appropriate rhetoric but conveying that they are consummating themselves in the decisive moment. An intellectual tragic hero of this kind should possess and retain the last word—an exalted bearing befitting any tragic hero, but with the added weight of a profound utterance. Through this final word, an intellectual tragic hero achieves immortality before their death, whereas an ordinary tragic hero attains immortality only after their demise.

Socrates serves as an example of an intellectual tragic hero. Upon hearing his death sentence, he dies instantly. Understanding that it takes immense strength of spirit to face death, and that the hero always dies before their actual demise, is crucial to grasping the essence of life. As a hero, Socrates is required to remain calm and composed, but as an intellectual hero, he must gather enough spiritual strength in the final moment to fulfill himself. He cannot solely focus on confronting death; he must swiftly transcend that conflict, asserting his selfhood. If Socrates had remained silent in the face of death, he would have weakened the impact of his life, casting doubt on whether his ironic resilience was a genuine primal strength or a game he played, exploiting its flexibility pathetically to sustain himself.

While what I have hinted at here may not entirely apply to Abraham, it reveals the necessity for him to fulfill himself in the final moment not through silent action but through having something to say. As the father of faith, Abraham holds absolute significance in terms of spirit. I cannot preconceive what he should say, but once he utters it, I can undoubtedly understand it and even understand Abraham himself in his words. However, this understanding does not bring me any closer to him than before. If Socrates had not provided a remark, I could have put myself in his position and created one, or a poet could have done so. But no poet can reach Abraham.

I must draw attention to the difficulty that lies in Abraham's ability to say anything at all. The paradox lies in his silence; Abraham is incapable of speaking. It is contradictory to demand that he speak, as it would require him to step out of the paradox, abandoning his role as Abraham and negating everything that came before. If, in the decisive moment, Abraham were to tell Isaac, "It is you who are to be sacrificed," it would be a sign of weakness. If he were capable of speaking, he should have done so earlier. The weakness lies in his lack of maturity and concentration to fully envision the magnitude of the pain beforehand, leaving some of it unconsidered and making the actual pain greater than anticipated. Furthermore, by engaging in such conversation, he would deviate from the paradox, and if he truly desired to speak to Isaac, he would have to transform his situation into a temptation. Otherwise, he would not be a tragic hero at all.

Nonetheless, a last word from Abraham has been preserved, and within that word, I can grasp his complete presence and understanding of the paradox. Primarily, he says nothing, and that is how he conveys his message. His response to Isaac takes the form of irony, as it is always ironic to say something and simultaneously not say it. Isaac asks because he assumes Abraham knows. If Abraham were to reply, "I know nothing," he would be speaking falsely. He cannot speak because what he knows cannot be articulated. Instead, he replies, "My son, God will provide himself a lamb for a burnt offering." In this response, we witness the double movement within Abraham's soul, as described earlier. If Abraham had simply renounced his claim to Isaac and nothing more, he would be uttering a falsehood. He knows that God demands Isaac's sacrifice, and he knows that he himself is ready to sacrifice him at that very moment. Therefore, having made this movement, Abraham is constantly performing the subsequent movement, acting on the strength of the absurd. In that sense, he speaks no falsehood, as, based on the absurd, it is possible that God might do something entirely different. However, he does not speak anything substantial; he speaks in a foreign language. This becomes even more evident when we consider that Abraham himself was the one to sacrifice Isaac. If the task had been different, if the Lord had commanded Abraham to take Isaac to Mount Moriah and let divine lightning strike him as the sacrifice, then Abraham's enigmatic speech would be appropriate, as he himself would be unaware of what would happen. But since the task is given to Abraham, he must act, and thus he must know at the decisive moment what he is about to do, understanding that Isaac is to be sacrificed. If he is not definitively aware of this, he has not completed the infinite movement of resignation. In that case, his words are not untrue, but he is far from being Abraham. He holds less significance than a tragic hero; he is merely an indecisive individual who cannot resolve to do either one thing or another, and therefore resorts to speaking in riddles. Such a wavering individual is nothing but a parody of the knight of faith.

It is possible to understand Abraham in this context, but only within the realm of the paradox. Personally, I can comprehend Abraham to some extent, but I recognize that I lack the courage to speak in the same manner, just as I lack the courage to act like Abraham. However, I do not suggest that his actions are insignificant due to this. On the contrary, they are remarkable and unparalleled.

What did his contemporaries think of this tragic hero? They viewed him as great and held him in high esteem. The subsequent generations, the noble assembly of worthies appointed as the jury to pass judgment on their predecessors, arrived at the same conclusion. However, none could truly understand Abraham. Yet, consider his accomplishment—to remain faithful to his love. One who loves God requires no tears, no admiration, and forgets their suffering in love. In fact, they forget so completely that not a trace of pain would remain if not for God's remembrance. For God sees in secret, knows the distress, counts the tears, and forgets nothing.

Therefore, either there exists a paradox where the individual, as an individual, stands in an absolute relation to the absolute, or Abraham is lost.

Epilogue

Is it necessary for us to employ the same strategy of self-deception that spice merchants used to inflate prices? Do we, in the realm of the spirit, require such tricks to convince ourselves that we have not yet reached the heights, just so we have something to occupy our time with? Or perhaps we have already perfected the art of self-deception. Is it a virtuosity in this skill that the present generation needs, or is it instead an honest seriousness that fearlessly and unwaveringly draws attention to our tasks? This honest seriousness should lovingly surround and protect our tasks, making them captivating and inspiring to noble minds. After all, noble natures are inspired by challenges. While each generation can learn from its predecessors, it can never learn the truly human element from them. In this regard, every generation begins anew, with the same task as the previous ones, unless they have shirked their duties and deceived themselves. This genuinely human element is passion, and through it, one generation can fully understand another and understand itself. No generation learns how to love from the previous one; each generation starts fresh, with no shorter task than its predecessor's. If someone, unlike the previous generation, is not content with love and seeks to go further, it is mere idle and foolish talk.

But the highest passion in a human being is faith, and no generation begins further than its predecessors in this regard, as each generation starts at the beginning. The succeeding generation does not surpass the previous one unless the latter has been faithful to its task and not betrayed it. Although it may seem wearisome, it is not for the generation to say. The task belongs to the generation, and it is irrelevant that the previous generation faced the same task, unless that particular generation or its individuals presume to occupy a position reserved only for the enduring spirit that governs the world. If a generation begins to do so, it becomes perverted, and it is no wonder that the entirety of existence appears perverted to them. Just as the tailor in the fairy-tale who reached heaven in his lifetime and looked down upon the world found life distorted. As long as the generation concerns itself with its task, the highest it can achieve, weariness is not a factor. The task is sufficient for a human lifetime. When children finish their games by noon during a holiday and impatiently ask for a new game, does it indicate that they are more advanced than children of the same or previous generations who could make their known games last the whole day? Or does it merely show that those children lack the good-natured seriousness inherent in play?

Faith is the utmost passion in a human being. While many individuals in every generation may not reach that point, none surpasses it. Whether others in our time discover this truth remains uncertain. From my own experience, I openly acknowledge that I have a long way to go. However, I do not wish to diminish the greatness of faith by reducing it to a trivial matter or a passing phase. Even if one fails to reach faith, life presents enough tasks, and if approached with honesty and love, it can still hold value, albeit incomparable to those who have attained a sense of the highest truth. Nevertheless, those who come to faith, regardless of their talents or simplicity, do not remain stagnant. In fact, they would be shocked if someone suggested otherwise. Just as a lover would protest if accused of standing still in their love, declaring, "I am not stagnant in my love, for it is my life." Yet, they do not progress towards something else. When they realize this, they seek another explanation.

The ancient desire to progress and move forward has always existed. Heraclitus, the enigmatic philosopher who recorded his thoughts and placed them in the Temple of Diana, considering them as his armor in life, stated, "One can never walk through the same river twice." His disciple, who sought to go beyond, added, "One cannot do it even once." Poor Heraclitus, to have such a disciple! This addition transformed Heraclitus' principle into an Eleatic doctrine that denied movement. However, the disciple's intention was not to regress to what Heraclitus had abandoned but to be a disciple who ventured further.

The Absolute Paradox

Kierkegaard rejects the idea of a proof of God's existence.

The idea of proving the existence of anything is absurd; one always starts with existing things and then attributes properties to them; not the other way around.

It is a difficult matter to prove that anything exists; and what is still worse for the intrepid souls who undertake the venture, the difficulty is such that fame scarcely awaits those who concern themselves with it. ... Thus I always reason from existence, not towards existence, whether I move in the sphere of palpable sensible fact or in the realm of thought. ... The procedure in a court of justice does not prove that a criminal exists, but that the accused, whose existence is given, is a criminal.

This is the fallacy in the attempt to infer the existence of God from his attributes – that is, the argument from design. Such a proof would always be open to doubt, for "even if I began I would never finish, and would in addition have to live constantly in suspense, lest something so terrible should suddenly happen that my bit of proof would be demolished."

But [perhaps] between God and his works there exists an absolute relationship; God is not a name but a concept. Is this perhaps the reason that his essentia involvit existentiam? The works of God are such that only God can perform them. Just so, but where then are the works of God? The works from which I would deduce his existence are not immediately given. The wisdom of God in nature, his goodness, his wisdom in the governance of the world – are all these manifest, perhaps, upon the very face of things? Are we not here confronted with the most terrible temptations to doubt, and is it not impossible finally to dispose of these doubts?

There is the implication in this that the belief in God is a leap of faith. In other words, you just know that God exists. Knowing that God exists, one proceeds to interpret one's experience in terms of that existence – not the other way around.

Even in a rational (deistic) proof of God's existence, then, there would be a leap of faith. The faith might manifest itself in a conviction in the logic of the argument. Prior to completing the argument, you are in doubt, after making the final step, you attain to certainty, between the two stages there is a gap, and that gap is bridged by faith.

Whilst this article does not discuss this point explicitly, it implies that logic cannot be taken as a given. Even the validity of logical arguments needs faith. So everything begins with faith. Faith is not some kind of supernumerary extra that is tagged onto the bulk of knowledge, a superfluous addition that we can well do without. Why place one's faith in logic? Why not directly in God?

And how does God's existence emerge from the proof? Does it follow straightway, without any breach of continuity? Or have we not here an analogy to the behaviour of these toys, the little Cartesian dolls? As soon as I let go of the doll it stands on its head. As soon as I let it go – I must therefore let it go. So also with the proof of God's existence. As long as I keep my hold on the proof, i.e., continue to demonstrate, the existence does not come out, if for no other reason than that I am engaged in proving it; but when I let the proof go, the existence is there. But this act of letting go is surely also something; it is indeed a contribution of mine. Must not this also be taken into account, this little moment, brief as it may be – it need not be long, for it is a leap.

Admittedly, this passage is opaque, but it appears to be saying that belief in God is a leap of faith, and that leap of faith is not conditioned by anything given in experience or thought. If you doubt of God's existence, you will doubt the logic that leads you his existence; if you believe in God, the leap of faith is all that is required.

Kierkegaard hints that the whole idea of starting out from a position of doubt (as Descartes claims to be able to do) and then proving God's existence is insincere.

Whoever therefore attempts to demonstrate the existence of God (except in the sense of clarifying the concept, and without the reservatio finalis noted above, that the existence emerges from the demonstration by a leap) proves in lieu thereof something else, something which at times perhaps does not need a proof, and in any case needs none better; for the fool says in his heart that there is no God, but whoever says in his heart to men: Wait just a little and I will prove it – what a rare man of wisdom is he! If in the moment of beginning his proof it is not absolutely undetermined whether God exists or not, he does not prove it; and if it is thus undetermined in the beginning he will never come to begin, partly from fear of failure, since God perhaps does not exist, and partly because he has nothing with which to begin.

The argument here is not wholly exact. The main point lies in the previous remark, that all proofs require an act of faith. The essence of Kierkegaard's approach to God is to deny any privileged status to a certain system. Science, for example, does not hold a privileged status of knowledge; pure reason and logical deduction require justification. Every system of belief, or individual creed, requires a leap of faith. The whole essence of the attack on faith, and the demonstration that it is a superfluous psychological reaction, is based on according another system a special status.

If no other system has such a special status, then the attempt to hold such a system up and work from there to the existence of God is either insincere or superfluous. The faith you repose in the system that proves God's existence is equivalent to the faith you have in God – the two stand and fall together. Therefore, if you advance such a proof, either you start with "nothing", in which case no proof is possible, or you start with the assumption that God does exist, in which case the proof is circular, or you are possibly doing something else – such as develop the concept of God, which may be equally unnecessary.

The correct procedure for Kierkegaard is to start with the belief in God, and then interpret experience in the light of that faith.

A project [of proving God's existence] would scarcely have been undertaken by the ancients. Socrates at least, who is credited with having put forth the physico- teleological proof of God's existence, did not go about it in any such manner. He always presupposes God's existence, and under this presupposition seeks to interprenetrate nature with the idea of purpose. Had he been asked why he pursued this method, he would doubtless have explained that he lacked the courage to venture out upon so perilous a voyage of discovery without having made sure of God's existence behind him. At the word of God he casts his net as if to catch the idea of purpose; for nature herself finds many means of frightening the inquirer, and distracts him by many a digression.